GARFIELD
DISCOVERS AMERICA

PIZZA IS FLAT...
THE WORLD IS ROUND!

Created by
JIM DAVIS

Written by Jim Kraft
Designed and Illustrated by Mike Fentz

EAU CLAIRE DISTRICT LIBRARY

Watermill Press

103083

B&T 10/25/94 $6.95

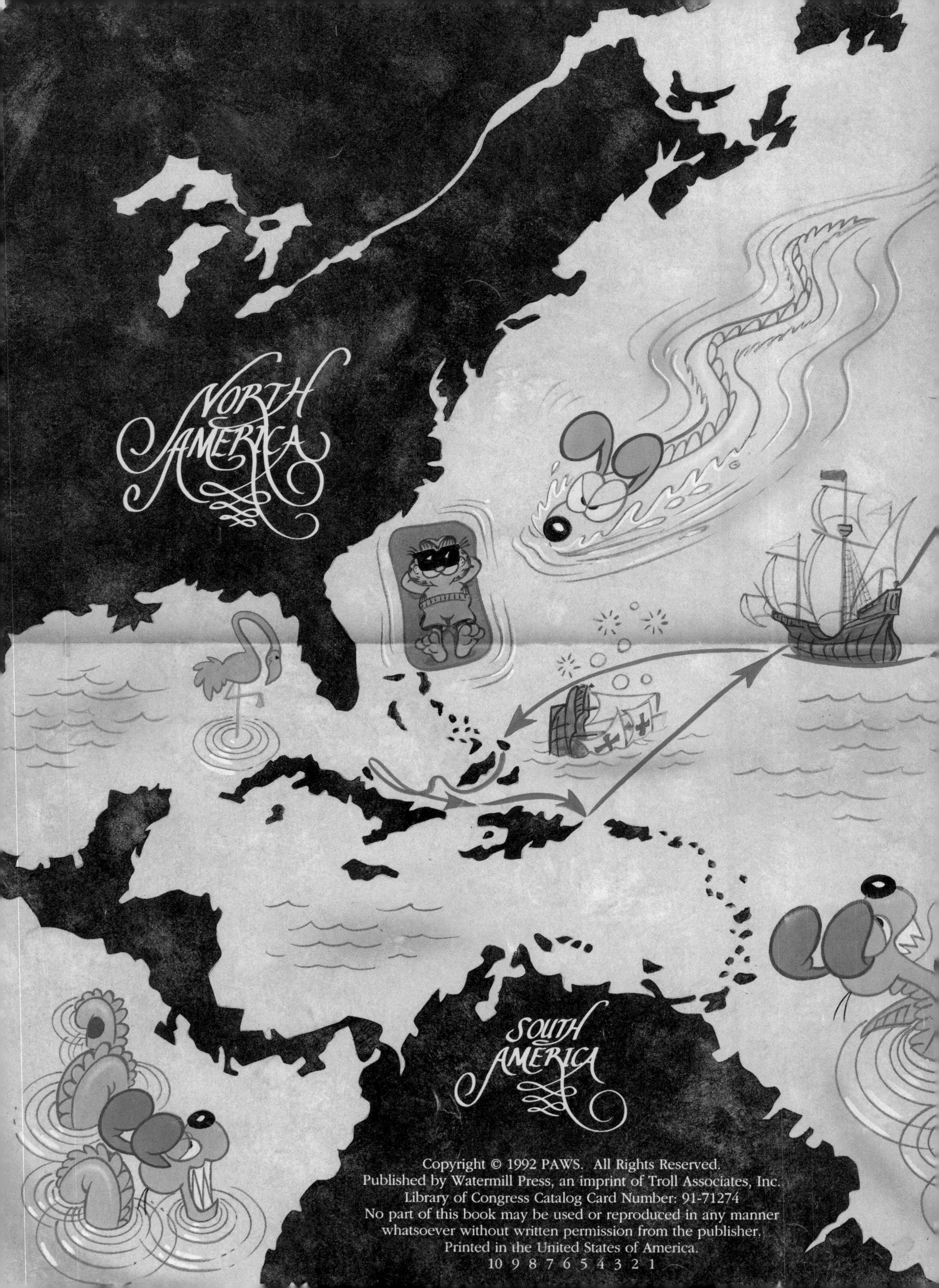
NORTH AMERICA
SOUTH AMERICA

Published by Watermill Press, an imprint of Troll Associates, Inc.
Library of Congress Catalog Card Number: 91-71274

Printed in the United States of America.
10 9 8 7 6 5 4 3 2 1

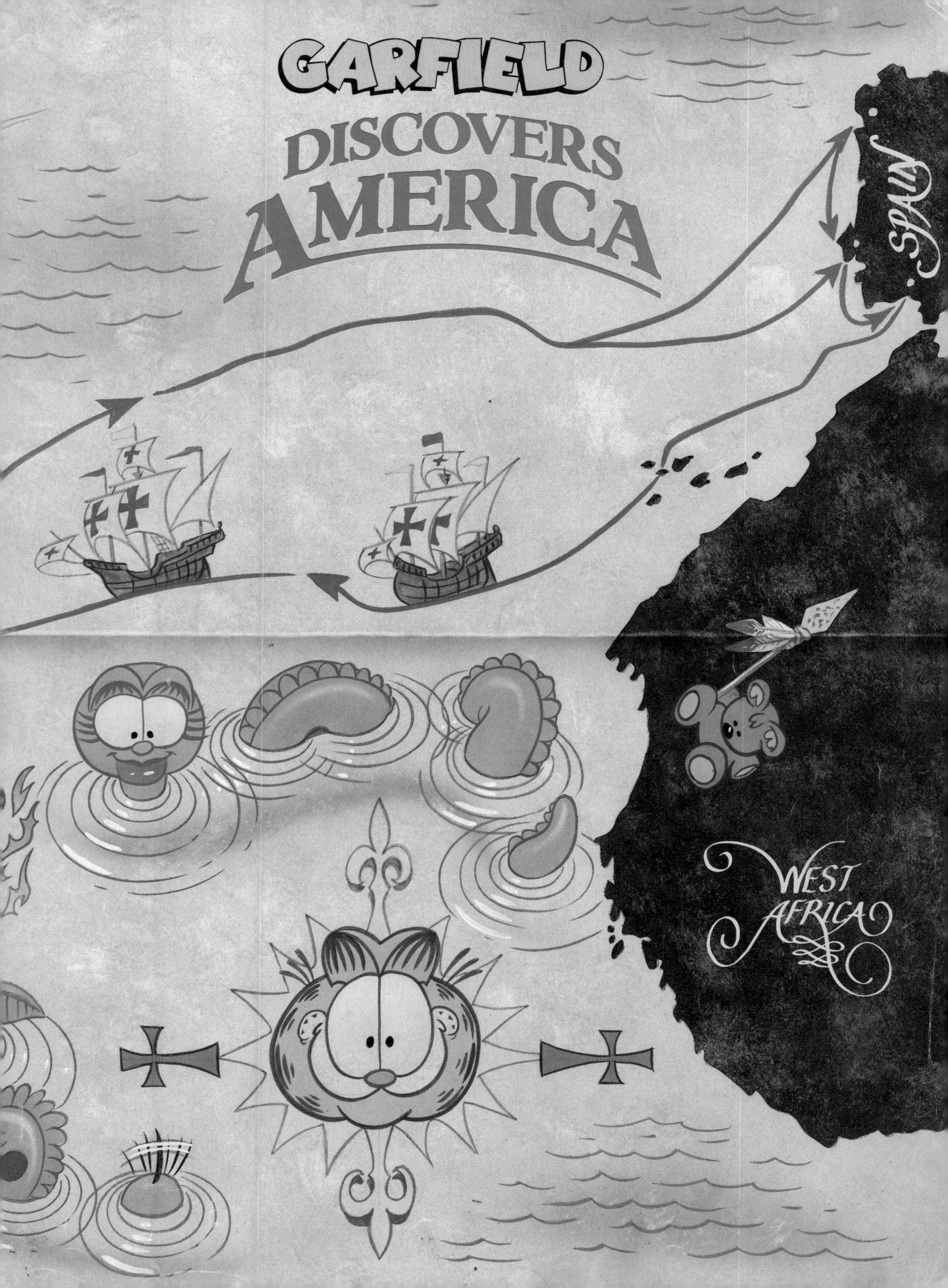
GARFIELD
DISCOVERS AMERICA
SPAIN
WEST AFRICA

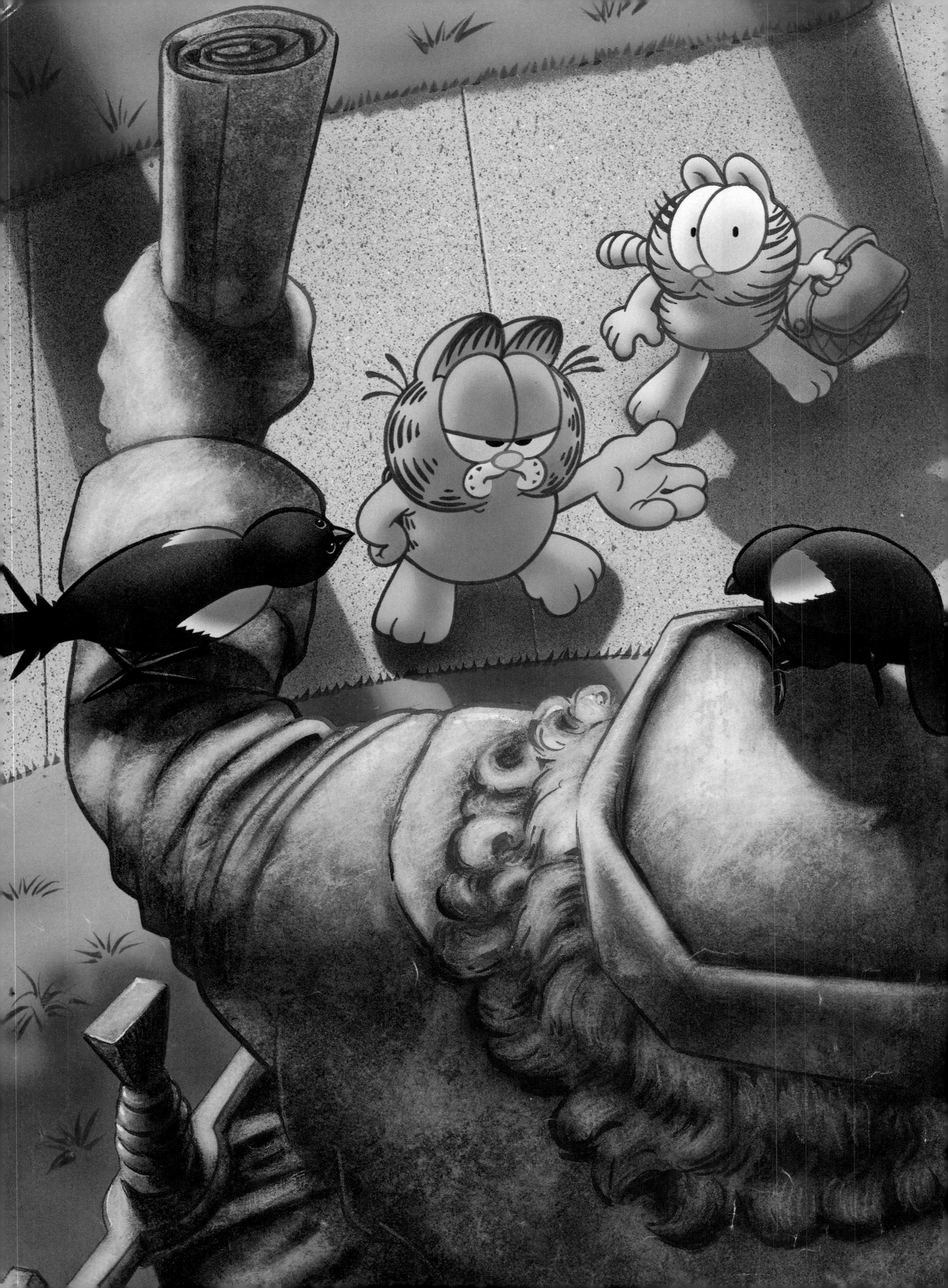

"Here's a good one, Nermal," said Garfield as they walked through Columbus Park one afternoon. "What has eight legs, two tails, and half a brain?"

"I don't know. What?"

"Two dogs!"

Suddenly Garfield stopped in front of the statue of Christopher Columbus. He frowned. "Discoverer of America? Ha!" Garfield shouted. "Without a cat, you'd be nowhere!" Then he resumed his walk.

"Garfield, what was that all about?" asked Nermal.

"I like to give Columbus a piece of my mind now and then."

"But why?"

"Because everyone thinks Columbus discovered America."

"Didn't he?"

"Nermal, let me tell you a little history . . .

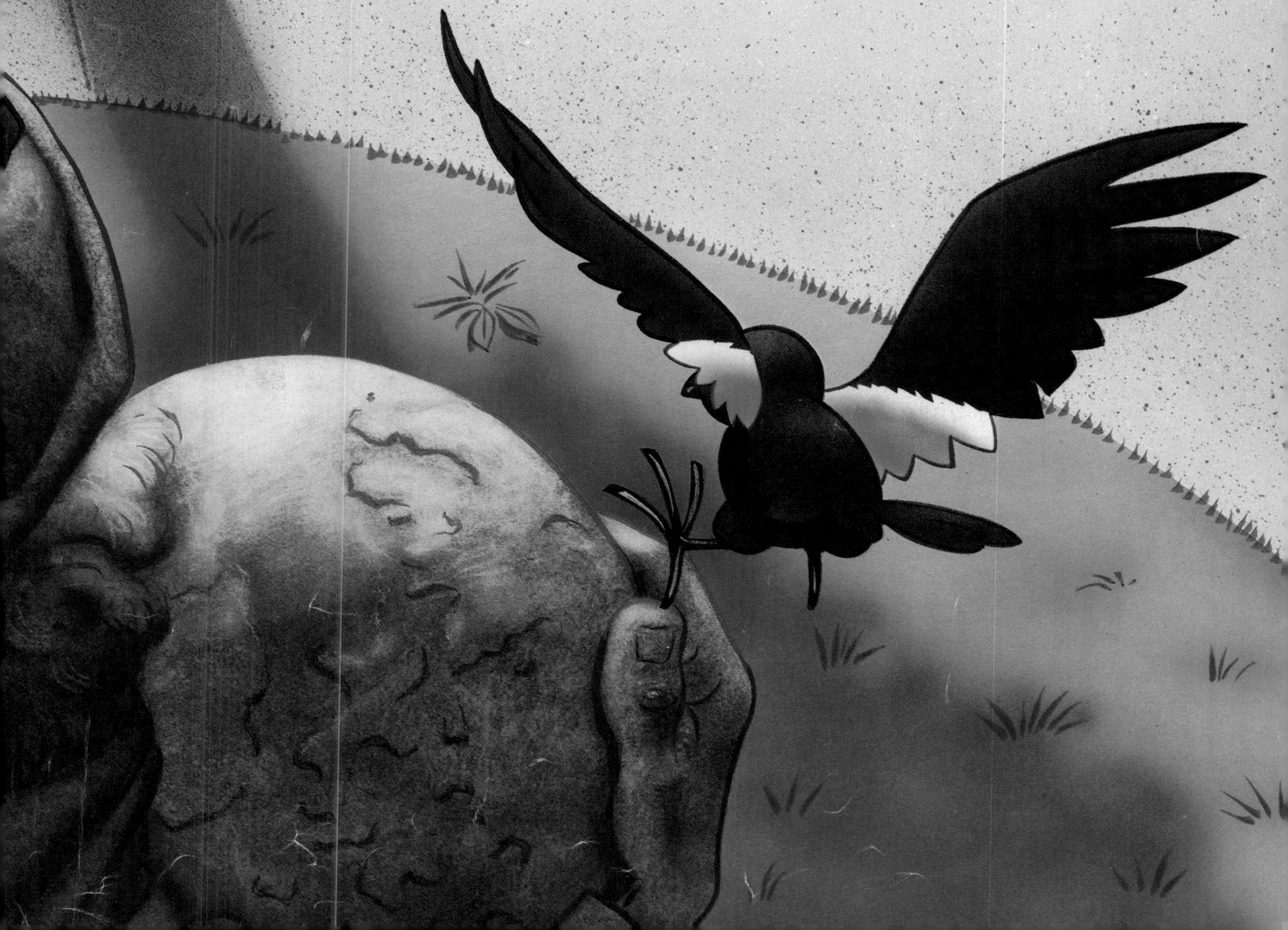

“Many, many years ago, near the end of the fifteenth century, my great-great-great-great-great uncle, Don Pedro Garfield, was the most important cat in Spain. For he was the Royal Mouser at the court of King Ferdinand and Queen Isabella.

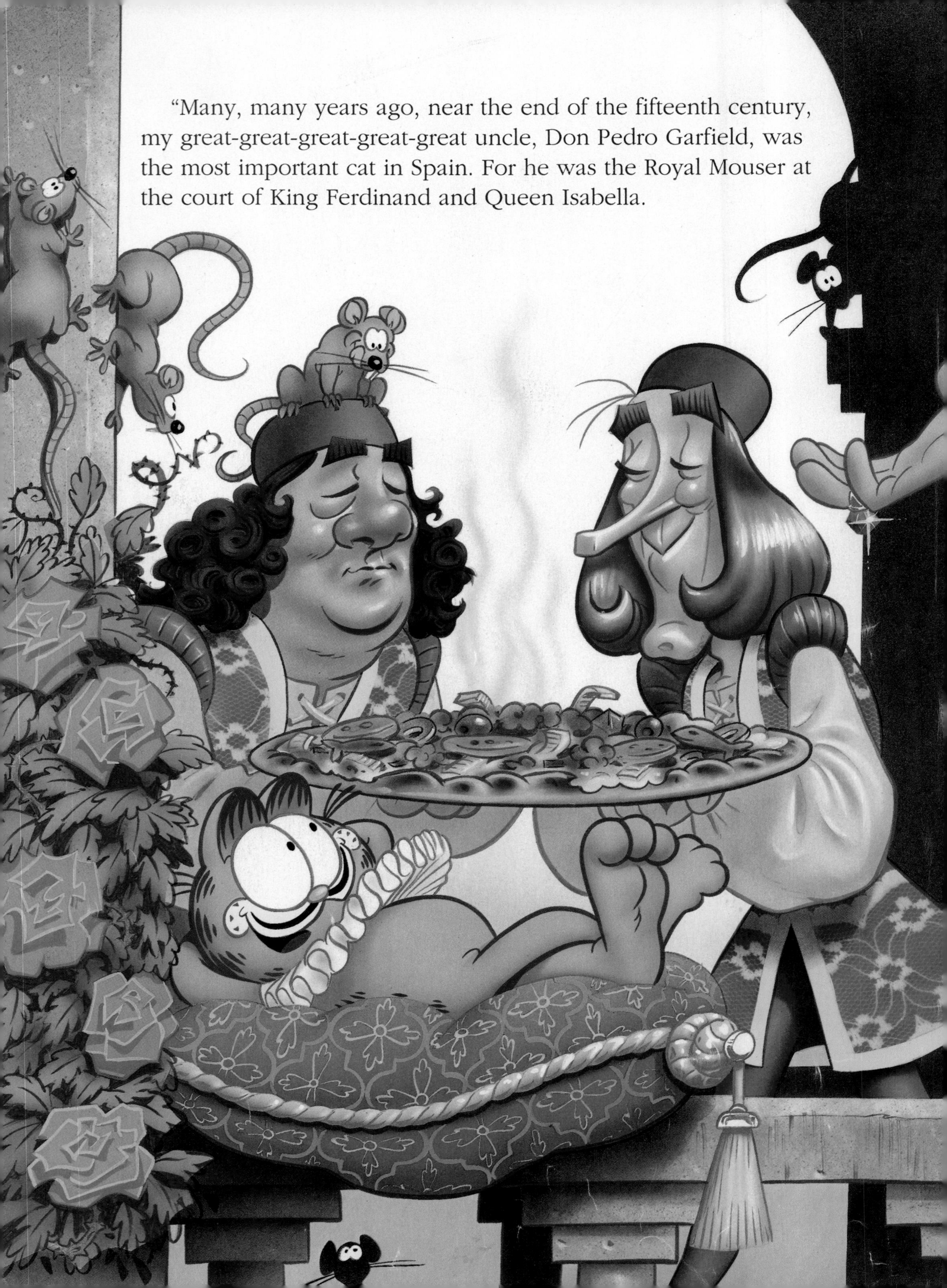

"Queen Isabella adored Don Pedro. King Ferdinand, however, was less impressed. 'That cat is the laziest creature in all Christendom!' the king would shout. 'While he sleeps, these mice are eating us out of castle and home!' "

"That's your relative, all right," said Nermal.

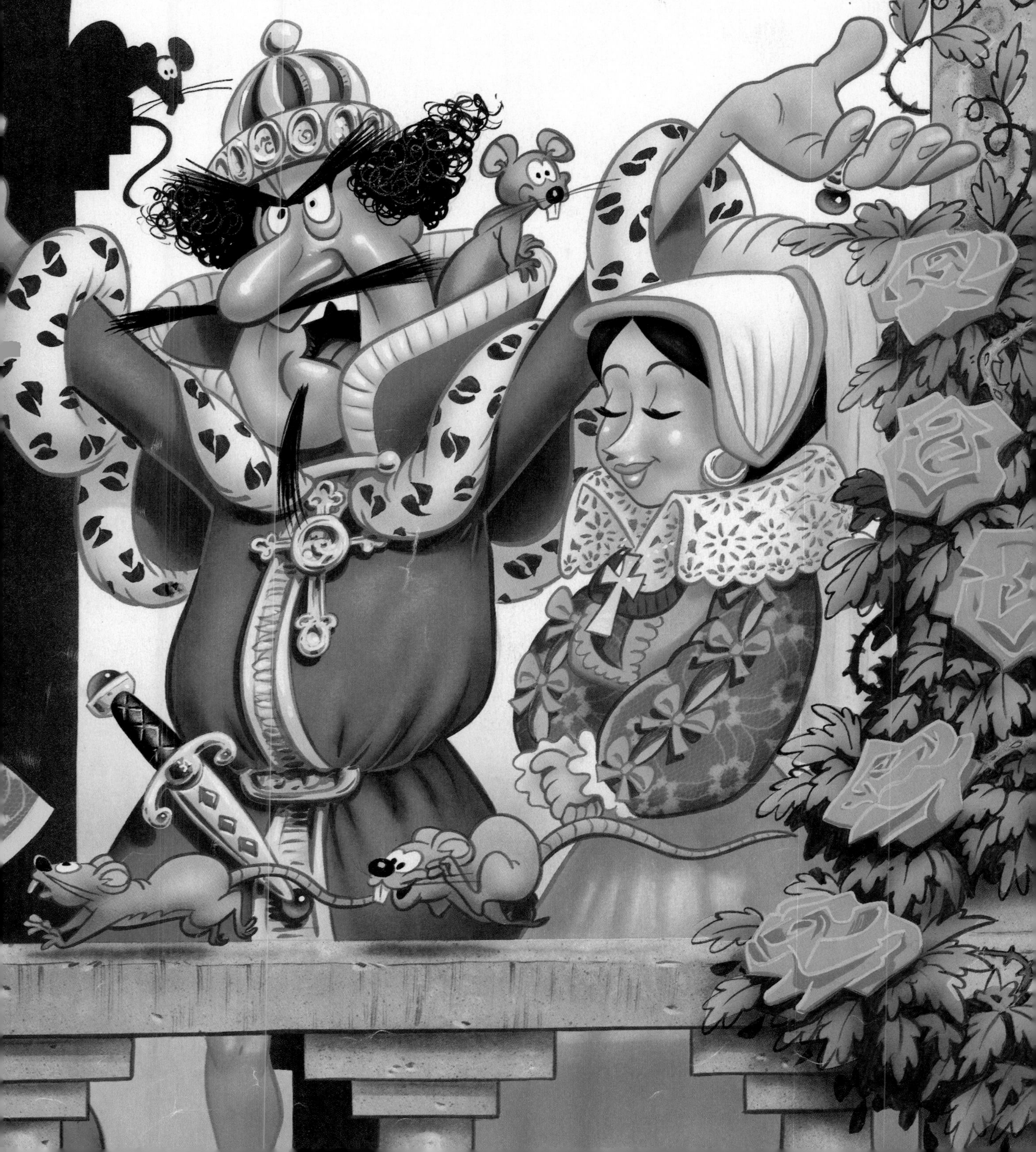

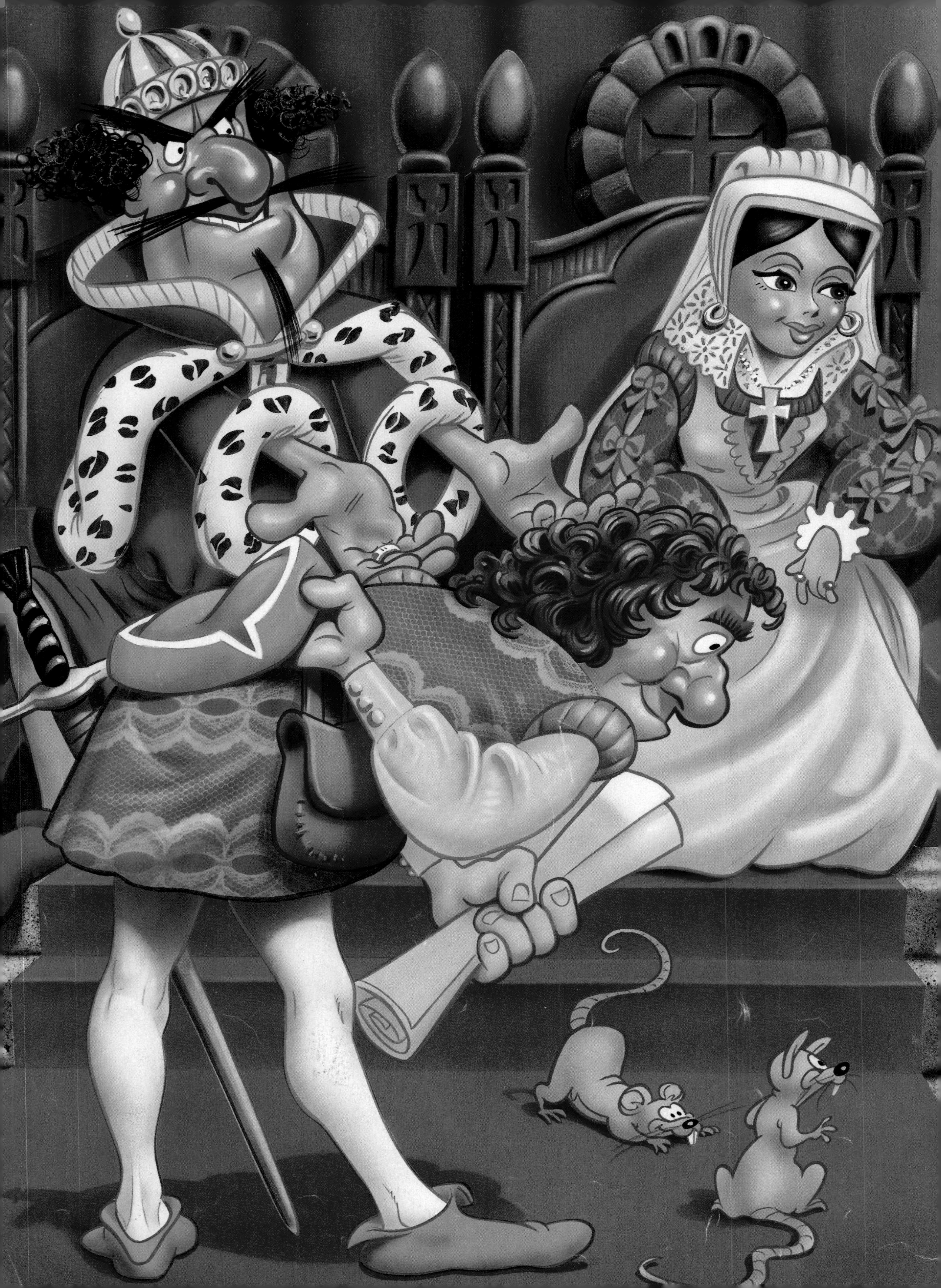

"One day, an Italian sailor named Christopher Columbus came to court. He had a plan to sail west from Spain over the Ocean Sea to the Indies, which is what Europeans called China and Japan in those days. No one had ever sailed west to the Indies. No one knew how wide the Ocean Sea was.

"Columbus needed ships and money. Queen Isabella seemed interested in his plan. But she could not help him right away. In fact, she kept him waiting for six years. Finally, in 1492, she summoned Columbus back to court.

" 'I like your plan,' said the queen. 'We will help you now.'

" 'We will not!' declared the king. 'His plan is preposterous.'

" 'You tell her, Ferdy,' added Don Pedro Garfield. 'If this guy wants to cruise, have him sail to Italy and bring us back some pasta.'

"Then the king's eye fell on Don Pedro, lazily munching sardines out of the king's spare crown. Ferdinand scowled.

" 'On second thought, we *will* pay for your voyage,' said Ferdinand. 'And to show our confidence in you, you may take the Royal Mouser along.'

"Don Pedro could barely contain his excitement. Or his lunch.

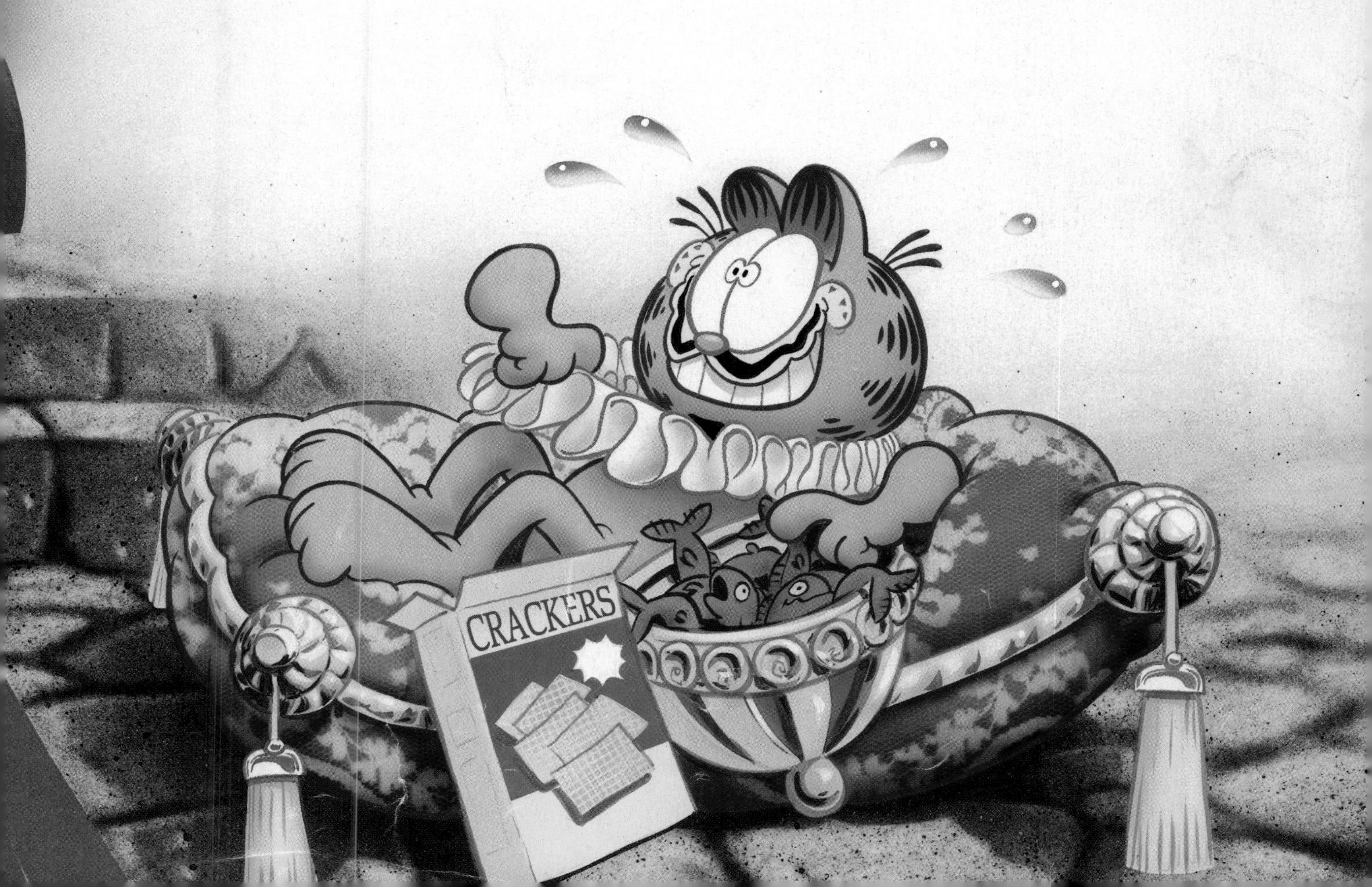
CRACKERS

"Ferdinand and Isabella gave Columbus three ships: the *Niña*, the *Pinta*, and the *Santa María*. Ninety sailors were hired. The ships were stocked with sea biscuits, salt meat, cheese, raisins, honey, and other foods.

"On August 3, 1492, the ships were ready to sail. Don Pedro Garfield was eager to go. He was given a military escort to the harbor.

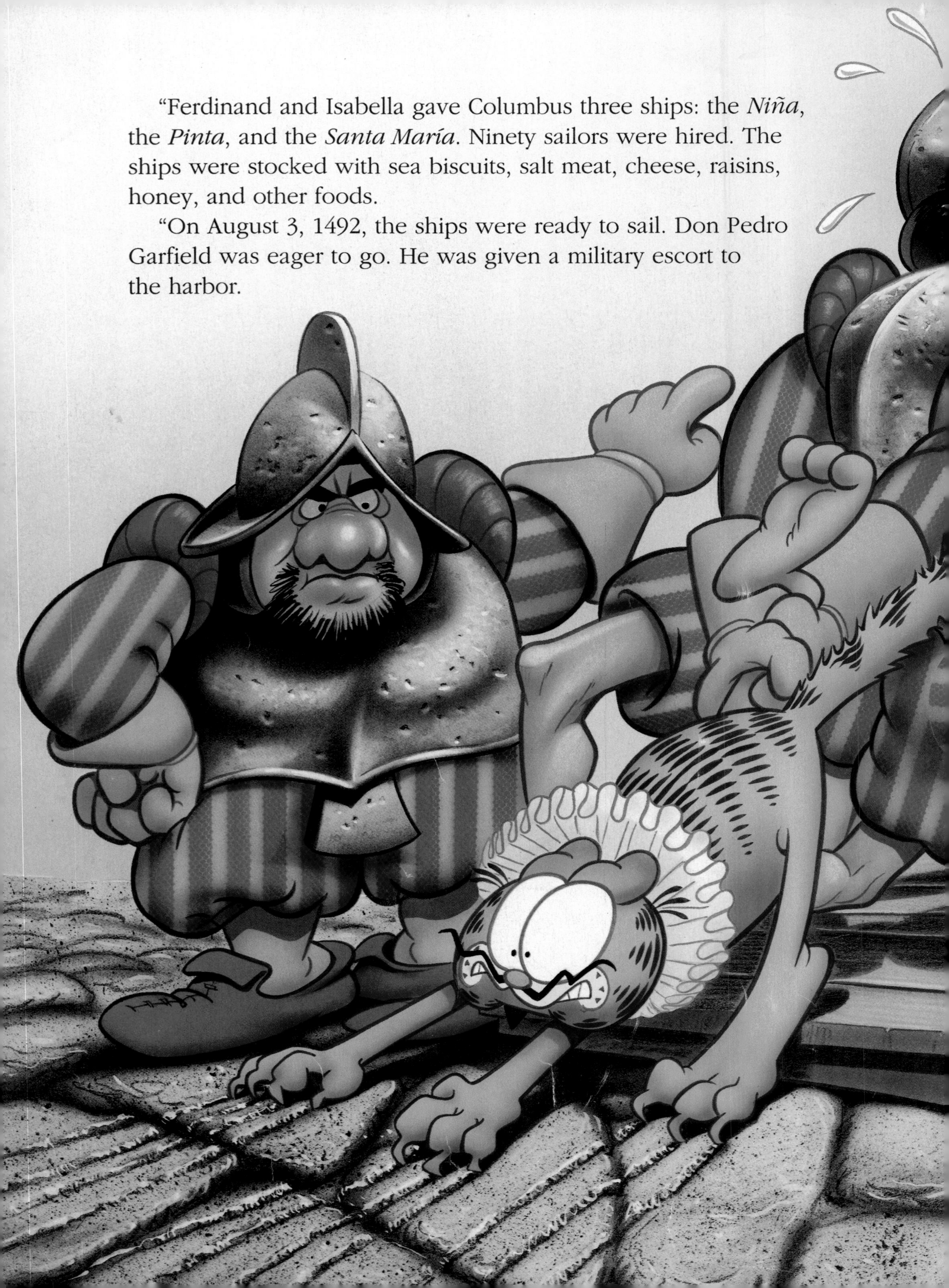

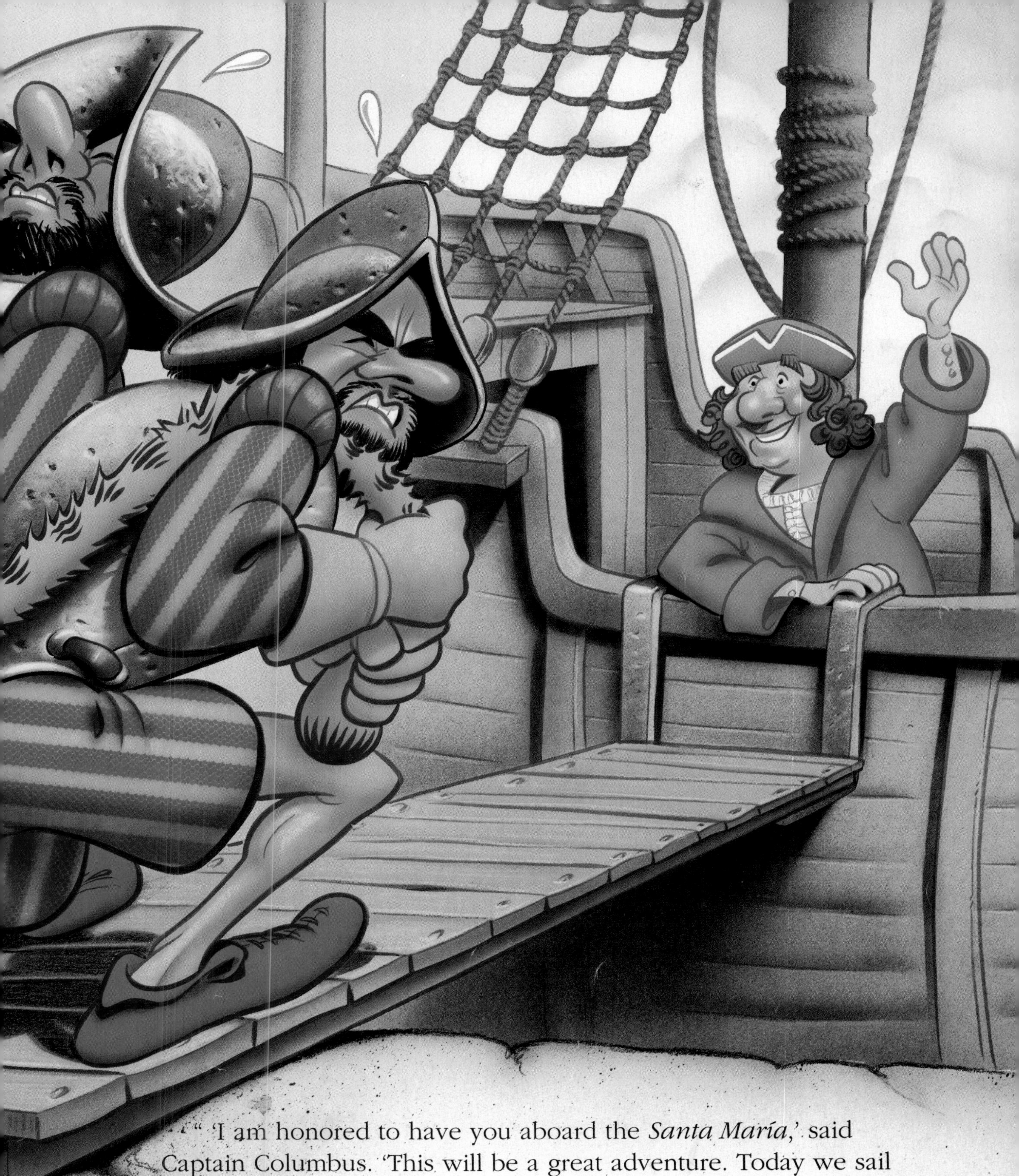

" 'I am honored to have you aboard the *Santa María*,' said Captain Columbus. 'This will be a great adventure. Today we sail into history!'

" 'Right,' Don Pedro replied. 'Well, if you need me, I'll be in my cabin, sobbing hysterically.'

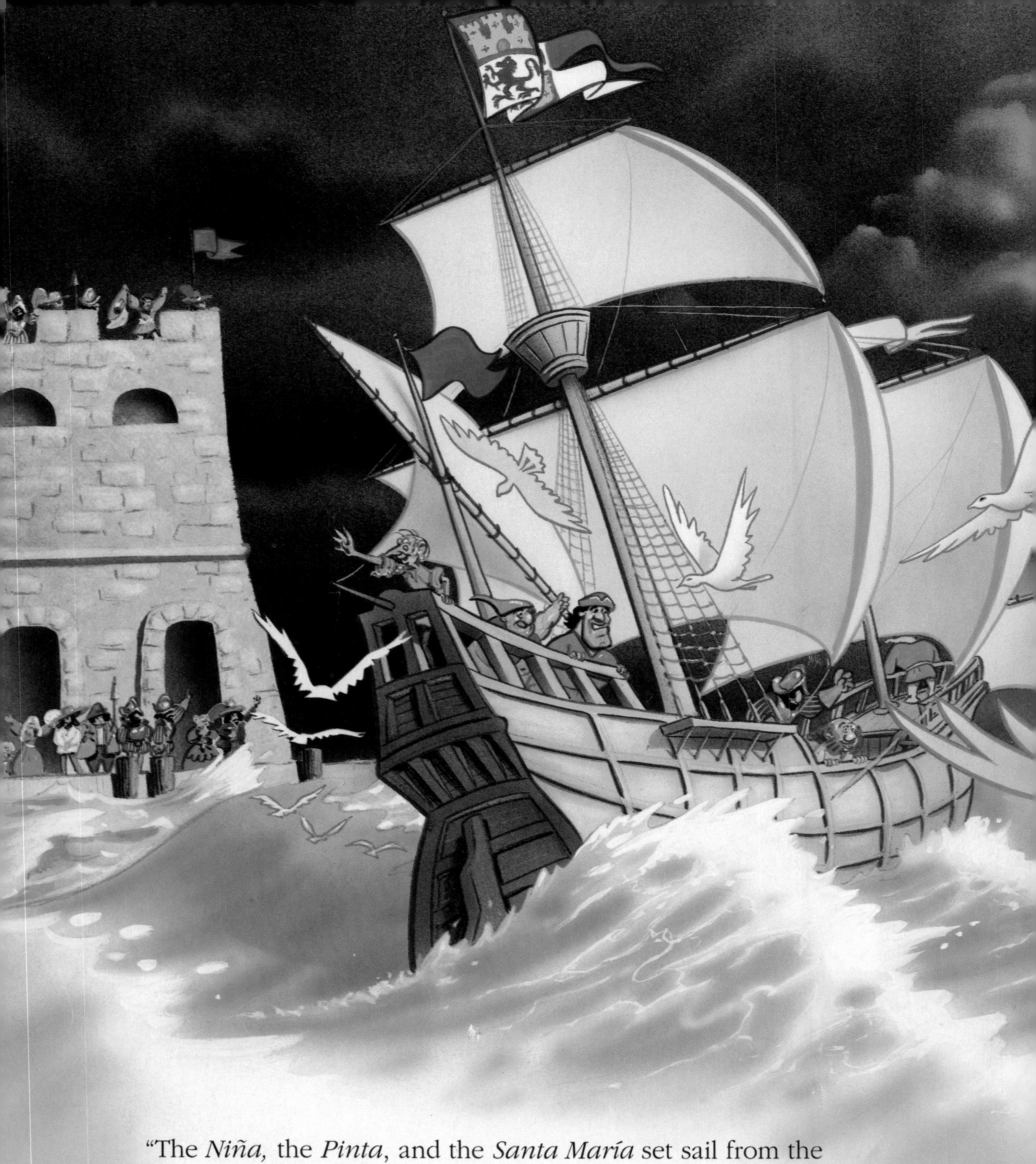

"The *Niña,* the *Pinta*, and the *Santa María* set sail from the Spanish port of Palos. No one knew when they would see Spain again. No one knew what dangers might be lurking over the horizon. No one knew the capital of North Dakota. But it was only the fifteenth century; there was a lot they didn't know.

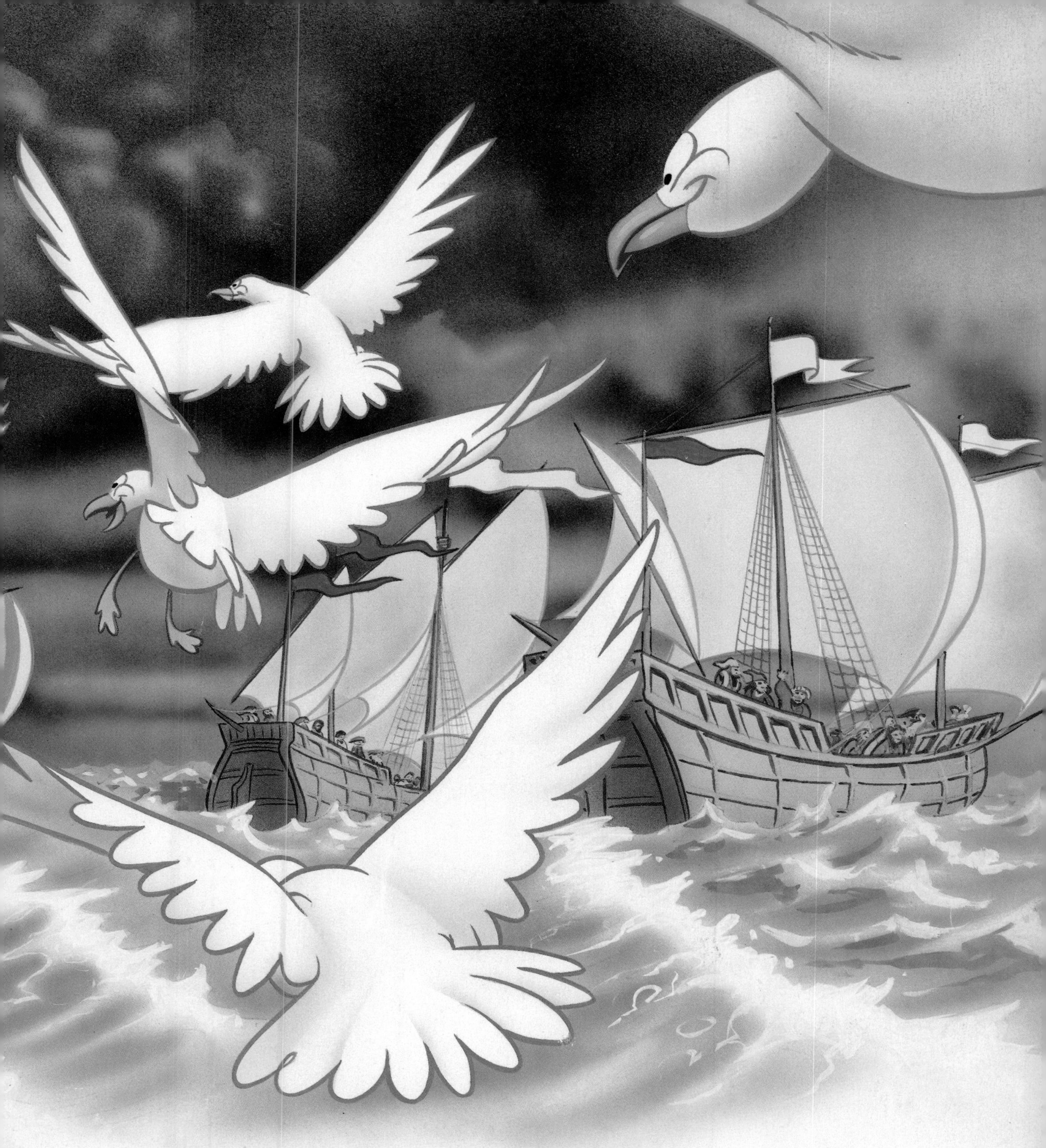

"The little fleet sailed first to the Canary Islands, where they stopped to take on a last load of supplies for the voyage. Don Pedro bought some anti-plague powder and a cookbook to read during the trip. Then, on September 6, the three ships headed west into the great Ocean Sea and the unknown.

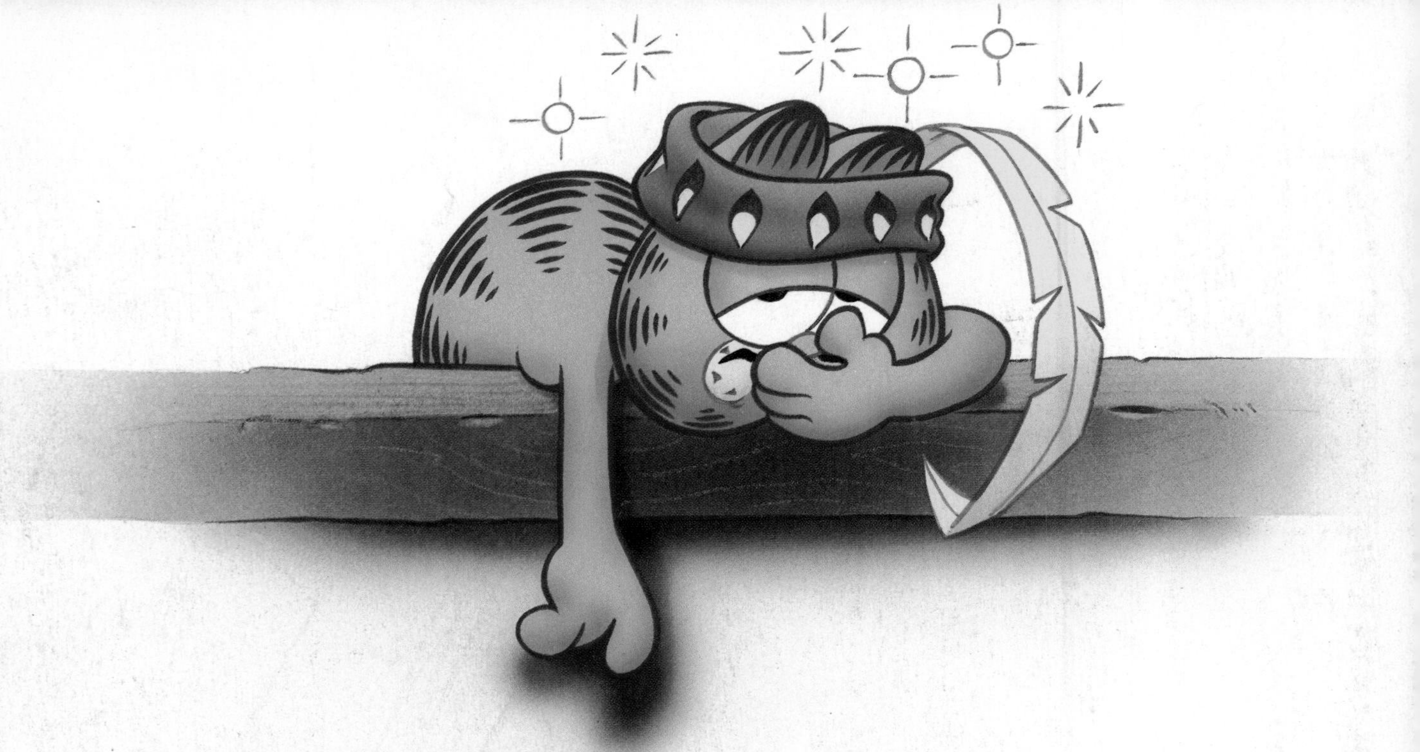

"Like all cats, Don Pedro was a natural sailor.

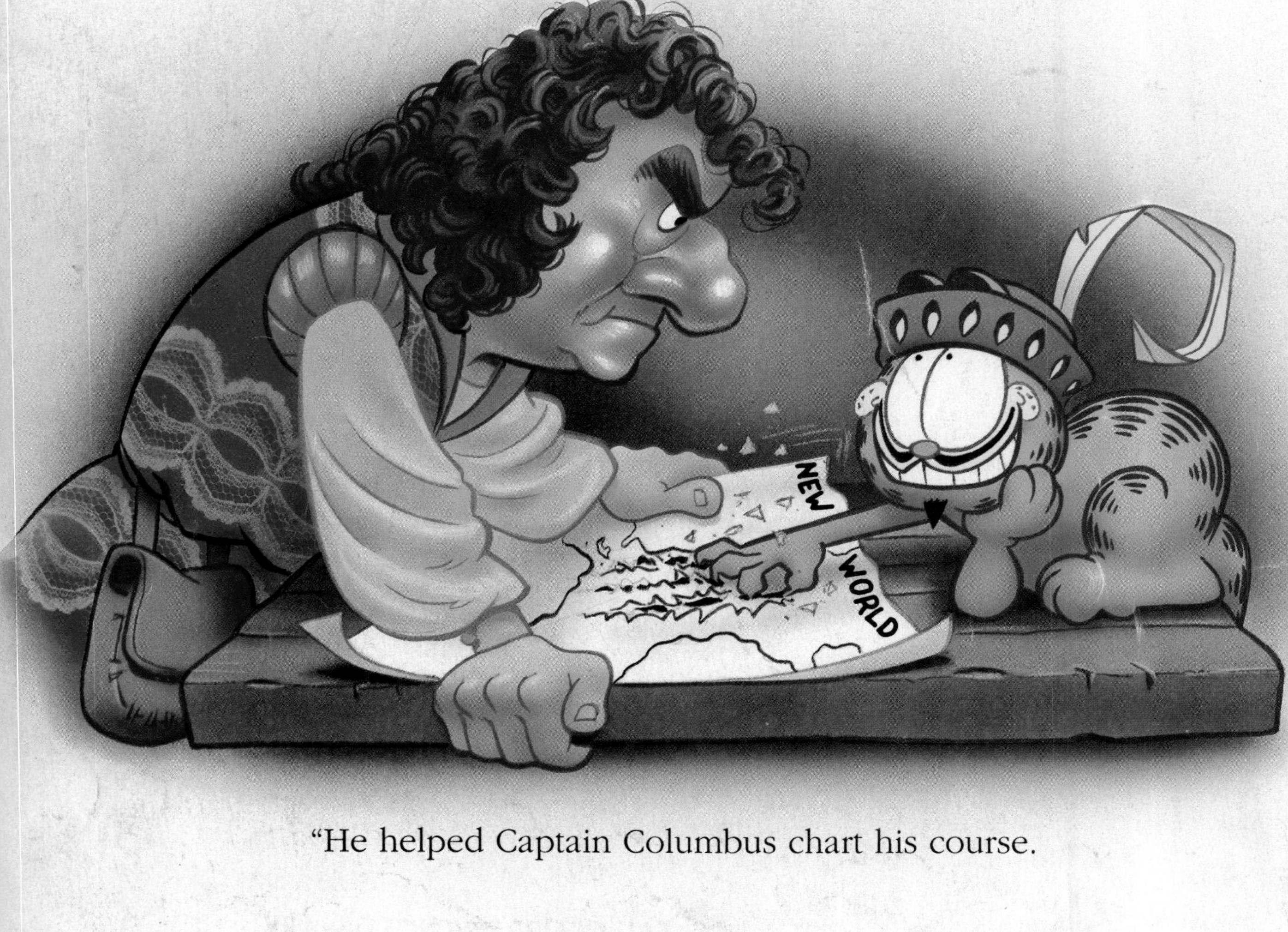
NEW
WORLD

"He helped Captain Columbus chart his course.

"And he made certain that the ship's rats did not eat all of the food.

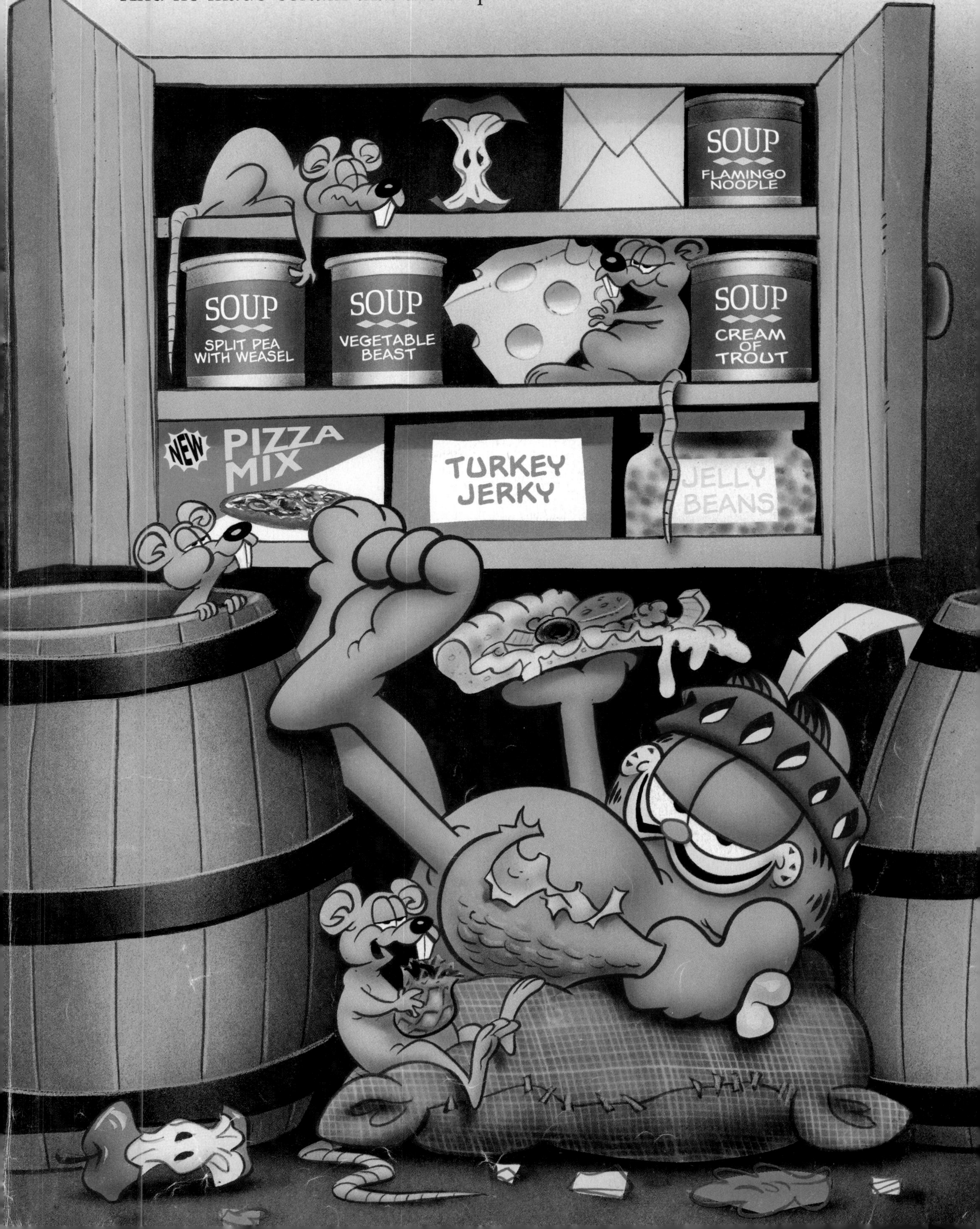
SOUP
FLAMINGO NOODLE
SOUP
SPLIT PEA WITH WEASEL
SOUP
VEGETABLE BEAST
SOUP
CREAM OF TROUT
NEW
PIZZA MIX
TURKEY JERKY
JELLY BEANS

"Each day the wind drove the ships farther and farther west. Still there was no sign of the Indies. But Columbus was not discouraged. 'Sail on! Sail on!' he would shout to the crew. 'The Indies must be just over the horizon.'

"The sailors, however, were getting nervous. What if the Ocean Sea was larger than Columbus thought? They might sail westward forever!

" 'There is only one thing to do,' declared one of the sailors. 'We must force Captain Columbus to turn back.'

" 'But that's mutiny,' said Don Pedro Garfield. 'It's against the law of the sea. The king and queen would never approve. As the royal representative, I cannot allow it.'

" 'We're nearly out of food,' stated another sailor.

" 'So what time's the mutiny?' Don Pedro asked.

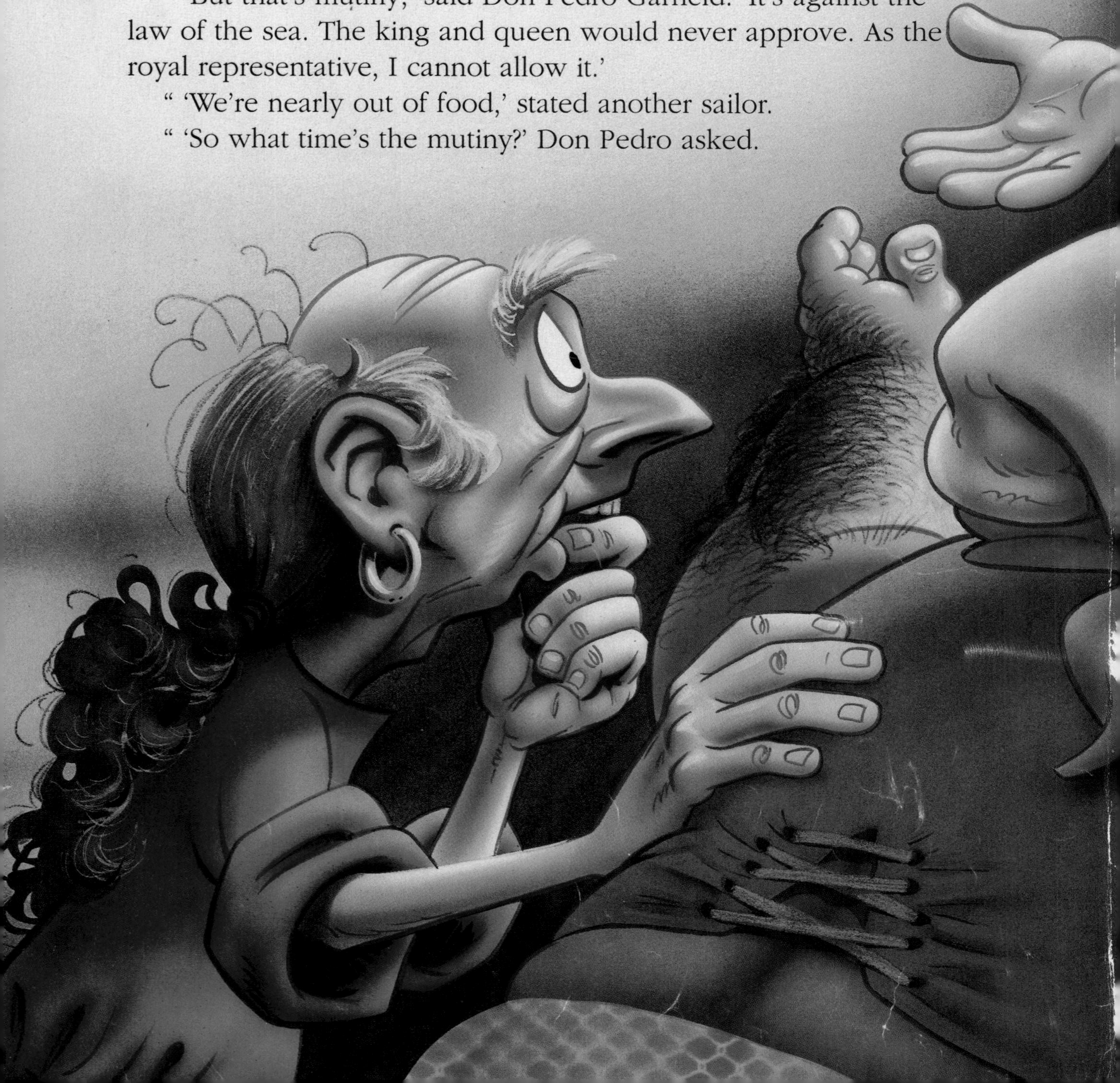

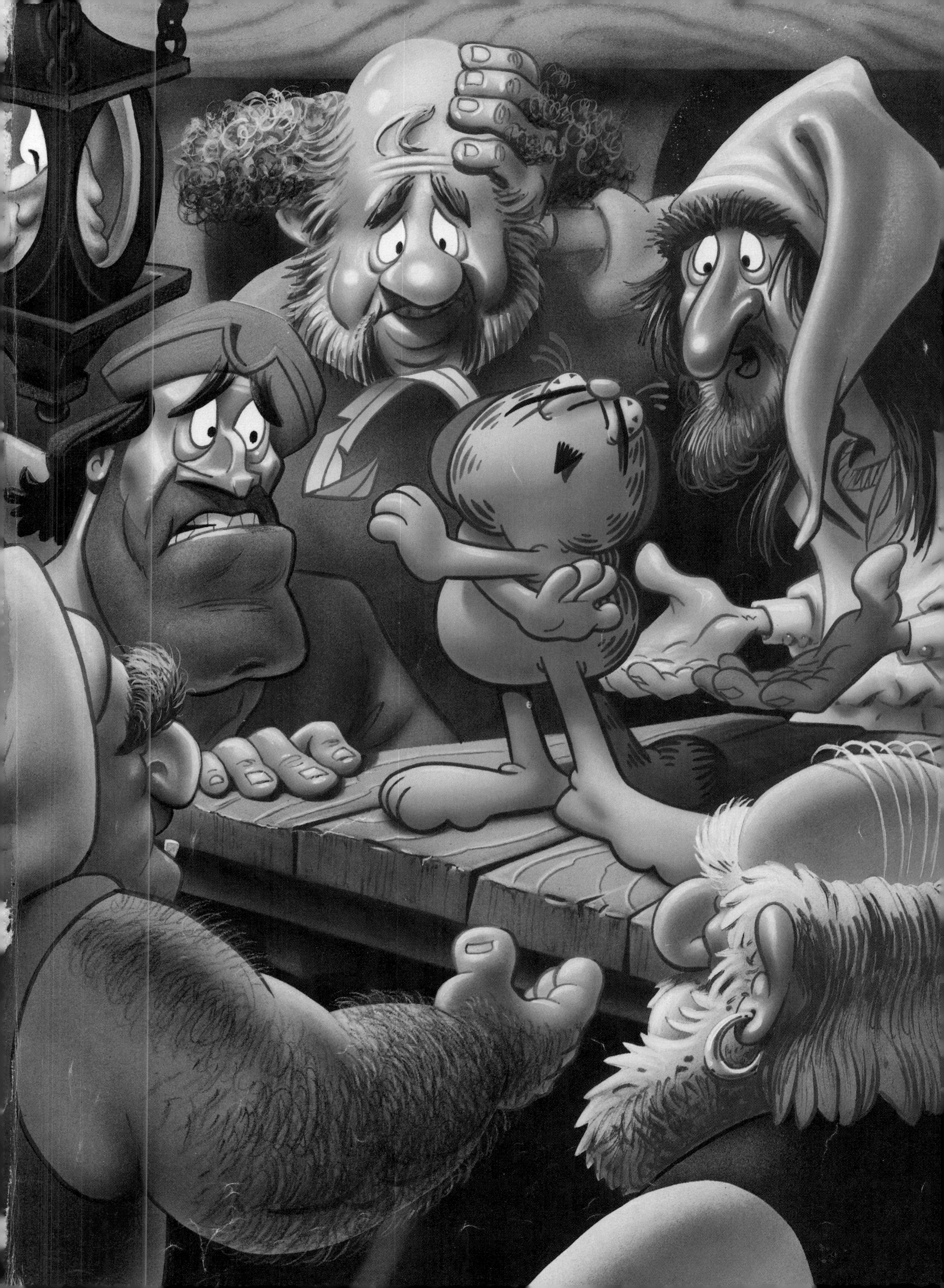

"On October 10 the crew confronted Columbus. 'Turn back now, before it's too late!' the sailors demanded.

" 'But we'll see the Indies in a few more days,' said Columbus.

" 'We don't want to see the Indies. We want to go home.'

" 'We're not kidding, Captain,' Don Pedro warned. 'Turn the ships around or we'll tell everyone that you sleep with the lantern on.'

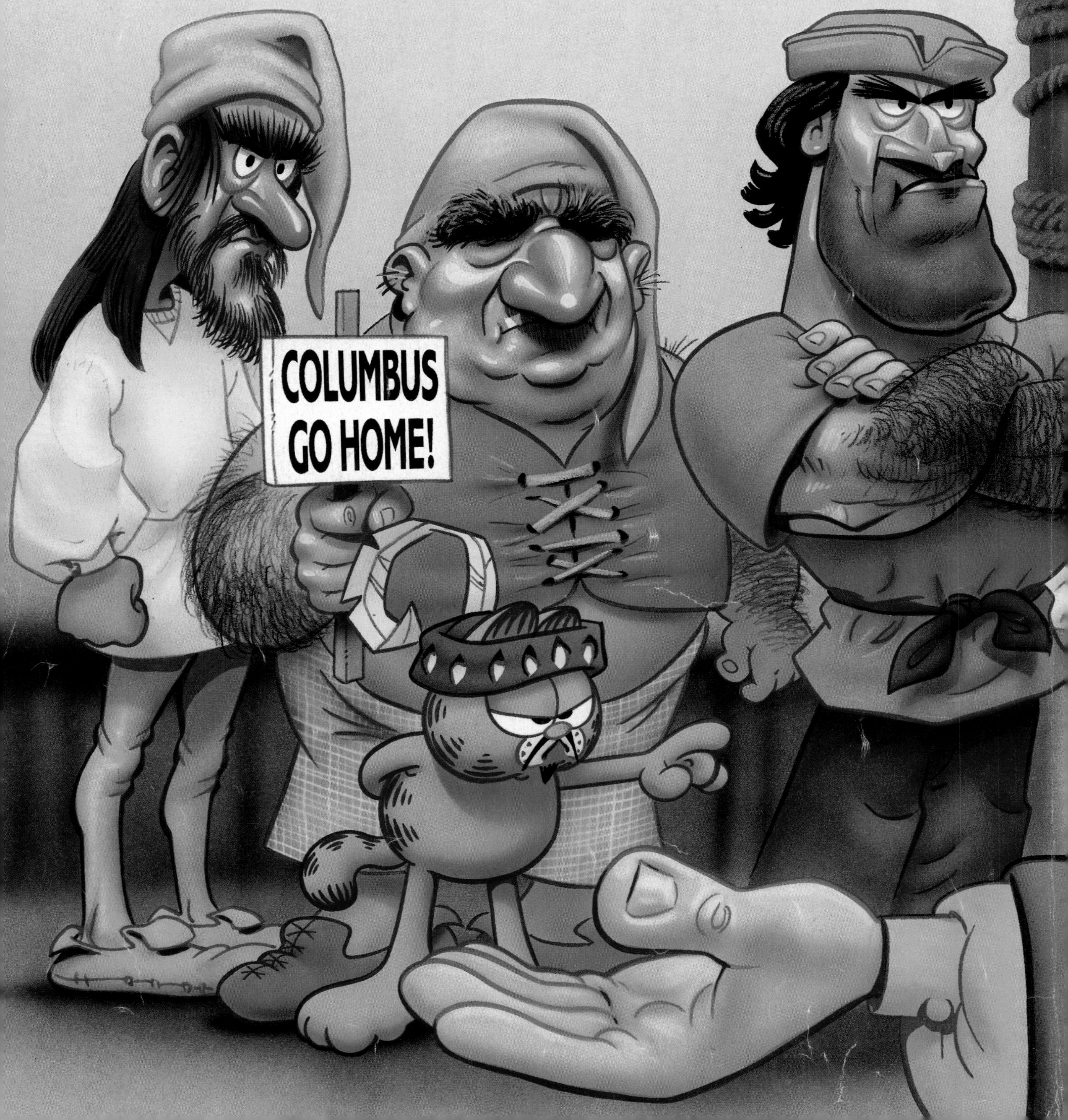
COLUMBUS GO HOME!

“ ‘And throw that fat cat overboard,’ the sailors continued. ‘He’s eaten everything on this ship except the anchor!’

“ ‘That’s a lie!’ shouted Don Pedro. ‘I ate the anchor last Tuesday!’

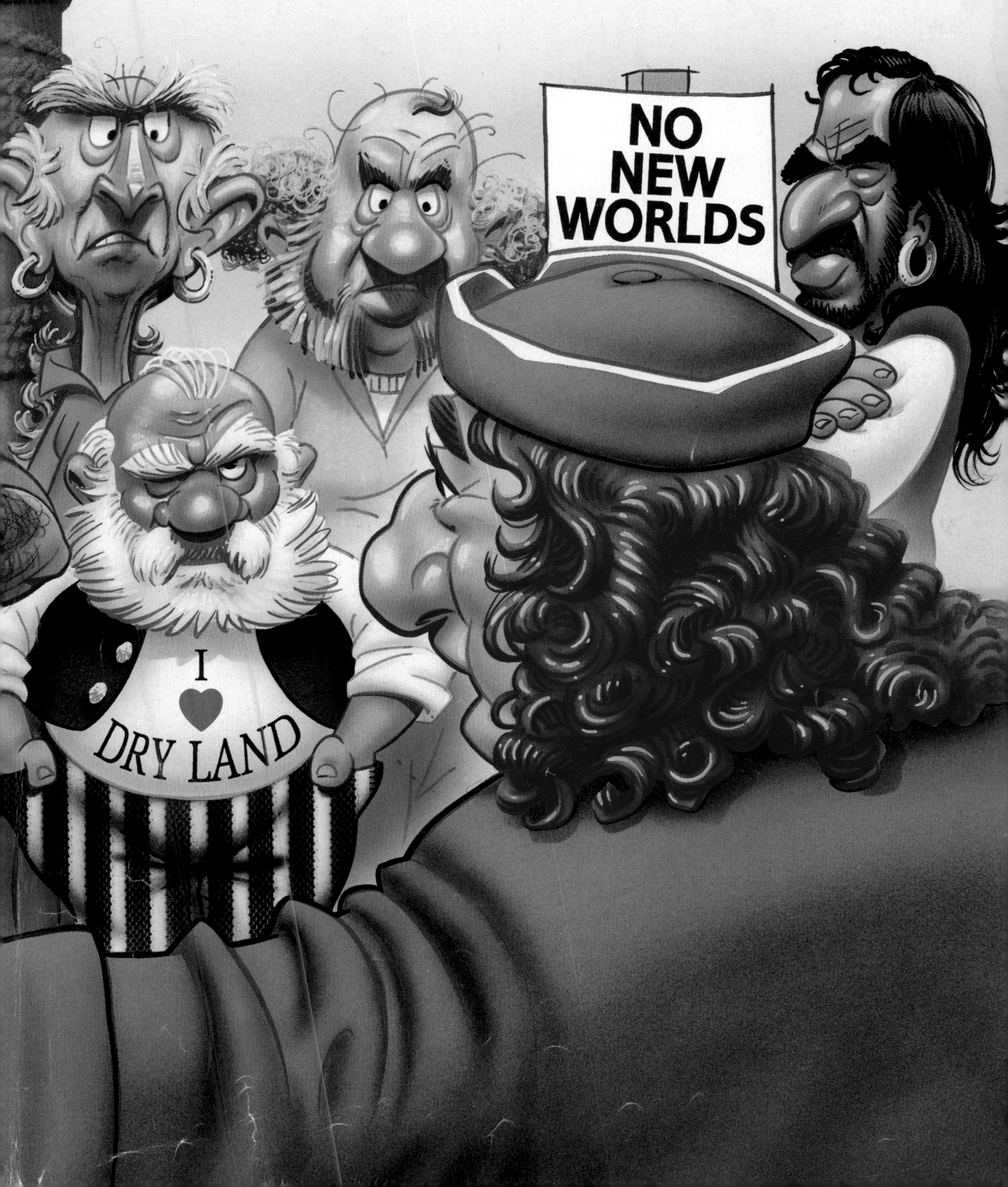
NO NEW WORLDS
I ♥ DRY LAND

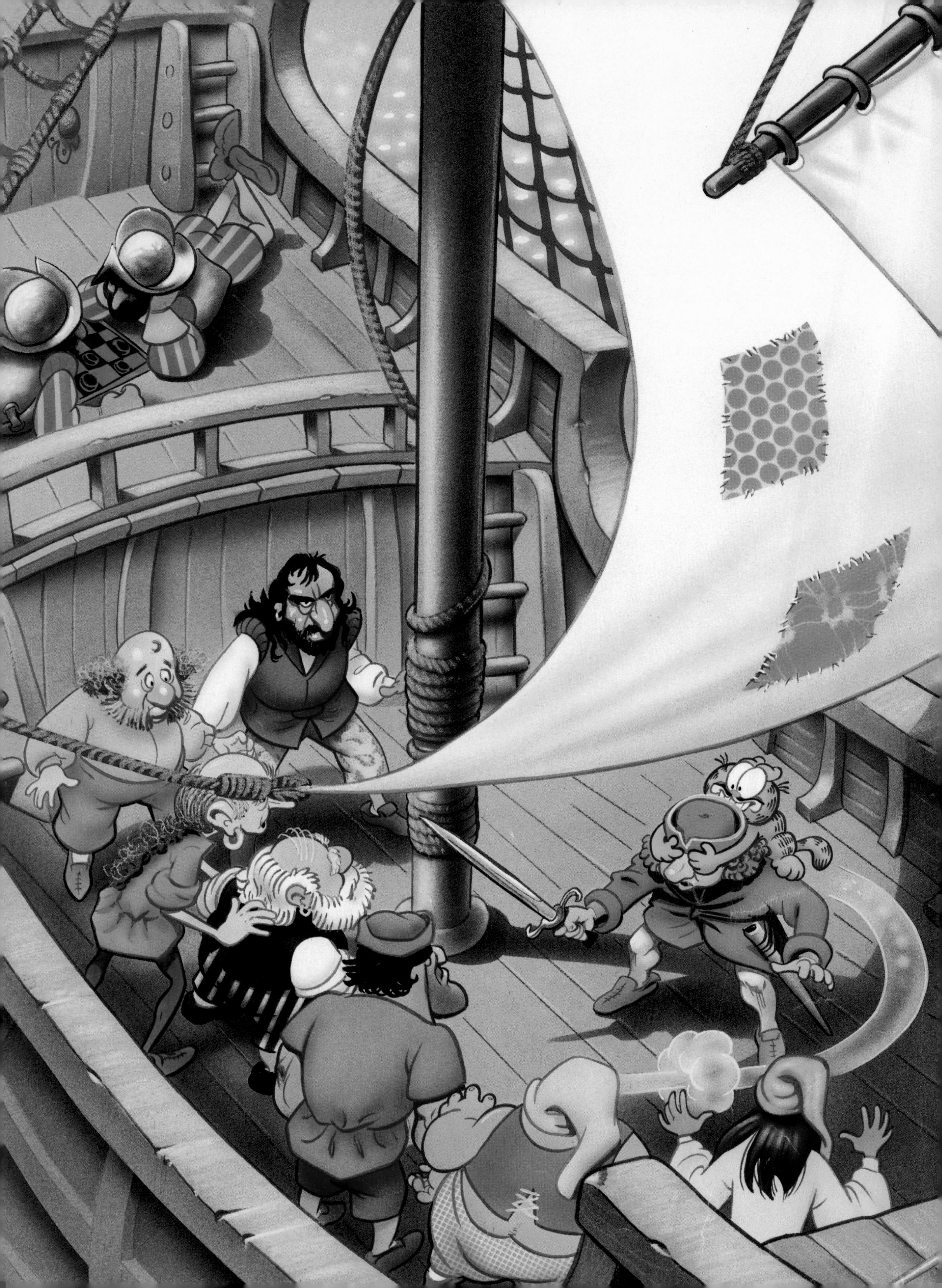

"The sailors lunged for Don Pedro, who leaped onto the shoulders of Columbus. Columbus snatched up a sword and together the cat and the captain faced the angry mob.

" 'This cat is royal property,' said Columbus. 'You must not harm him.'

" 'You tell 'em, Chris,' said Don Pedro Garfield. 'I'm behind you one hundred percent.'

" 'Give me three more days,' Columbus continued. 'If we don't reach the Indies in that time, I will turn back. And the cat goes on a diet immediately.'

"Everyone agreed to those terms, even Don Pedro, who was happy to sacrifice for the good of all, and showed it by his heroic whining.

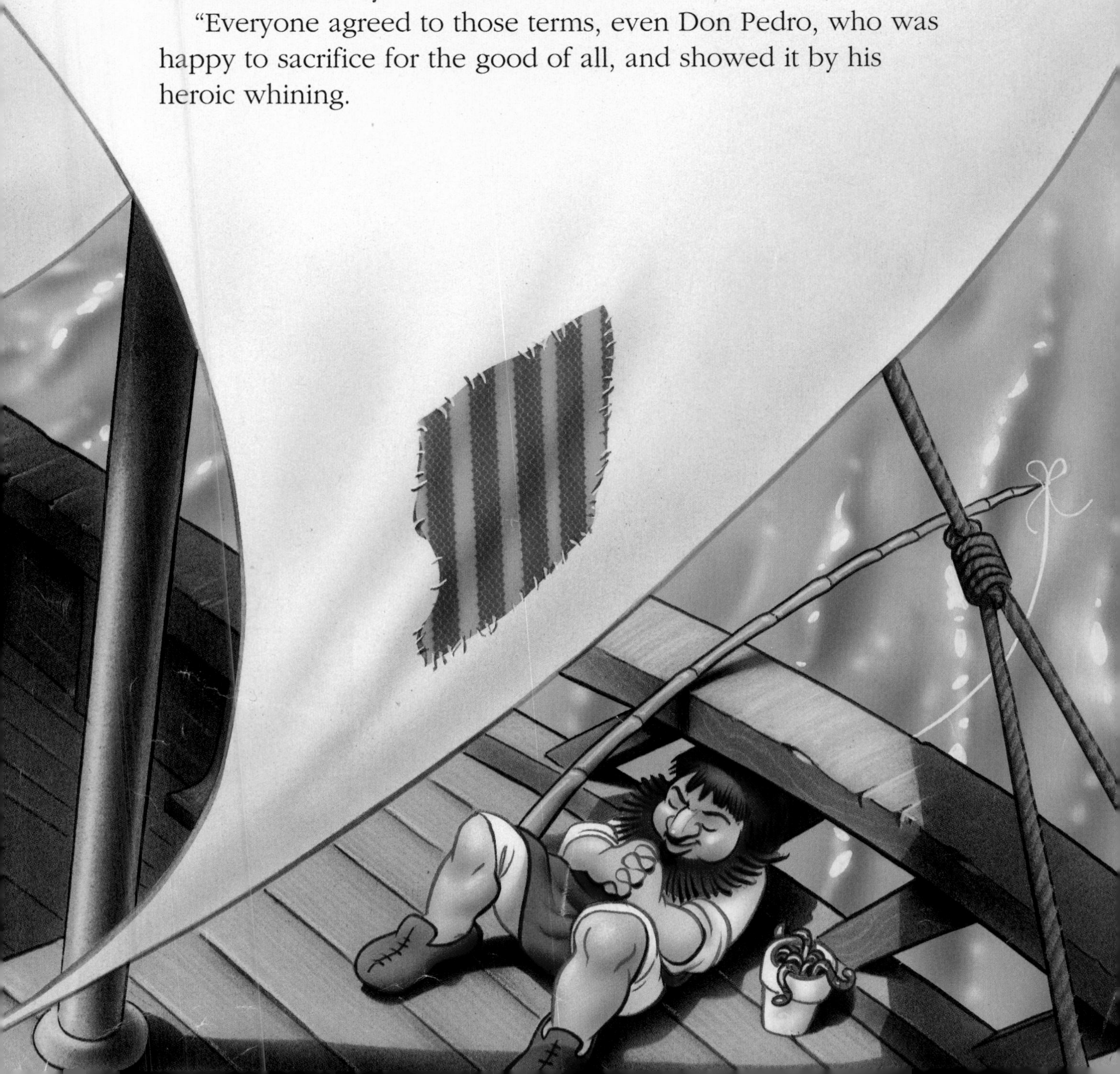

"The ships sailed on. By October 12 they had been at sea for thirty-seven days and had sailed more than two thousand miles.

"That morning, long before dawn, Don Pedro was awakened by his growling stomach. He dragged himself up on deck, where he clung weakly to the prow of the ship.

" 'I'm so hungry I could almost eat a mouse. Almost,' moaned Don Pedro.

"Don Pedro stared ahead. Black water and black sky stretched on forever. Then he blinked. Was something out there? He rubbed his eyes. There *was* something! Could it be? Yes, it was! It was . . .

". . . a huge slice of roast beef on a plate!

" 'Food ho!' cried Don Pedro. 'Man the knives and forks! We're saved!'

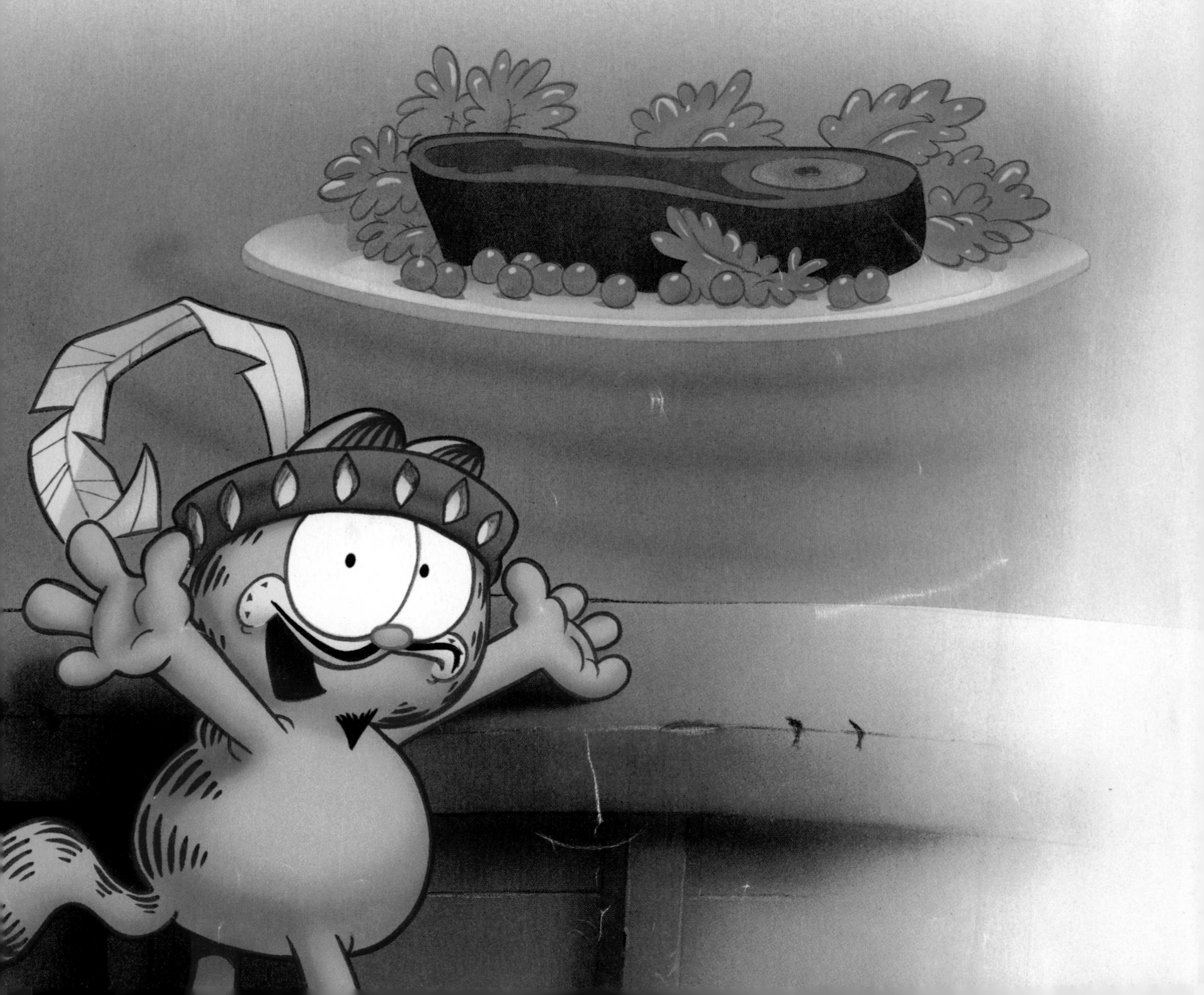

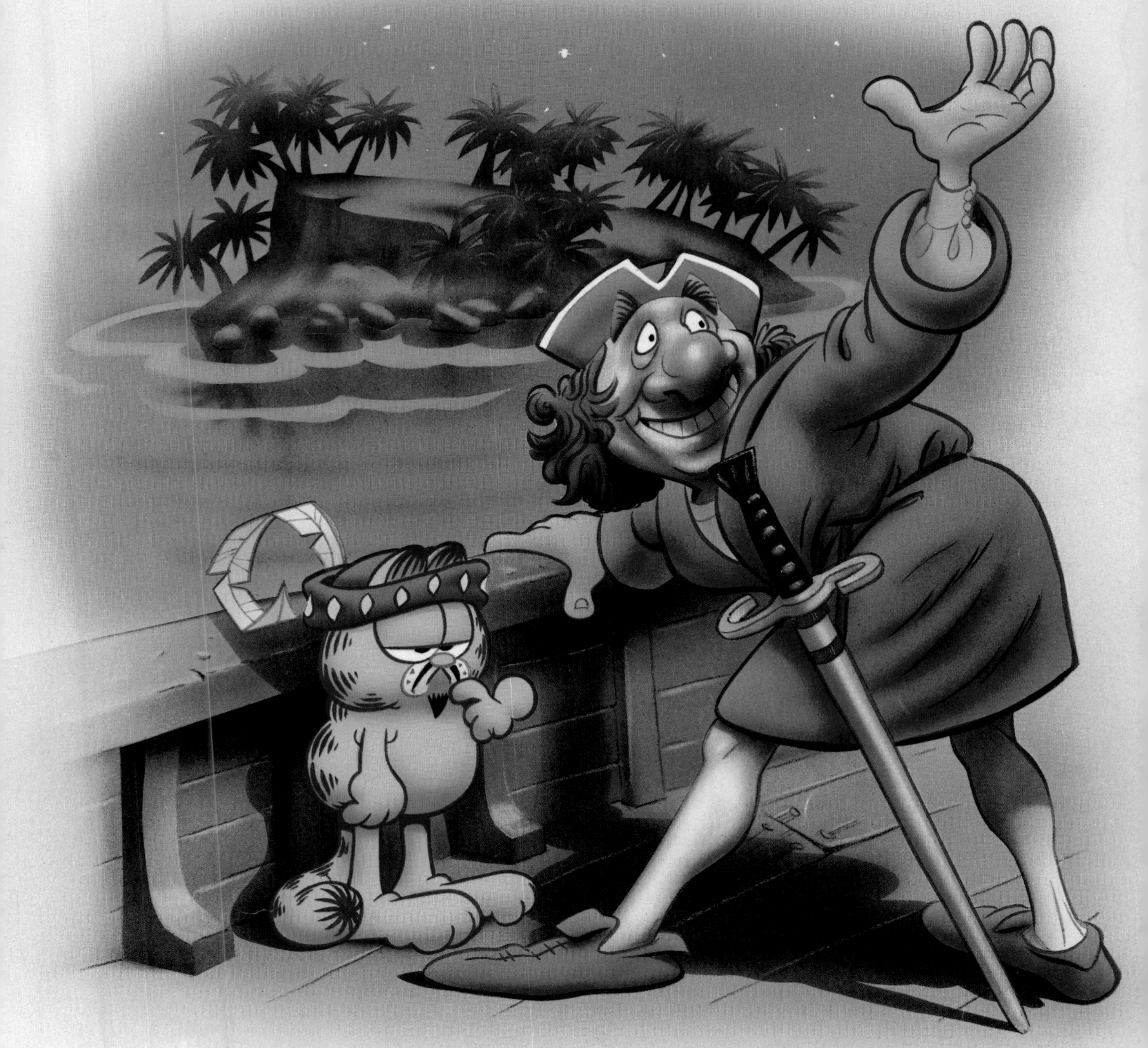

"Don Pedro Garfield fired a cannon to alert the *Niña* and the *Pinta*. Startled by the blast, Columbus and the crew scrambled on deck.

" 'Look there!' said Don Pedro, pointing.

" 'An island!' shouted Columbus. 'By San Fernando, we've done it! We've reached the Indies!'

" 'An island? The Indies?' said Don Pedro. 'Yes, of course! The Indies! That's what I saw. Now, what time do you think they open for breakfast?'

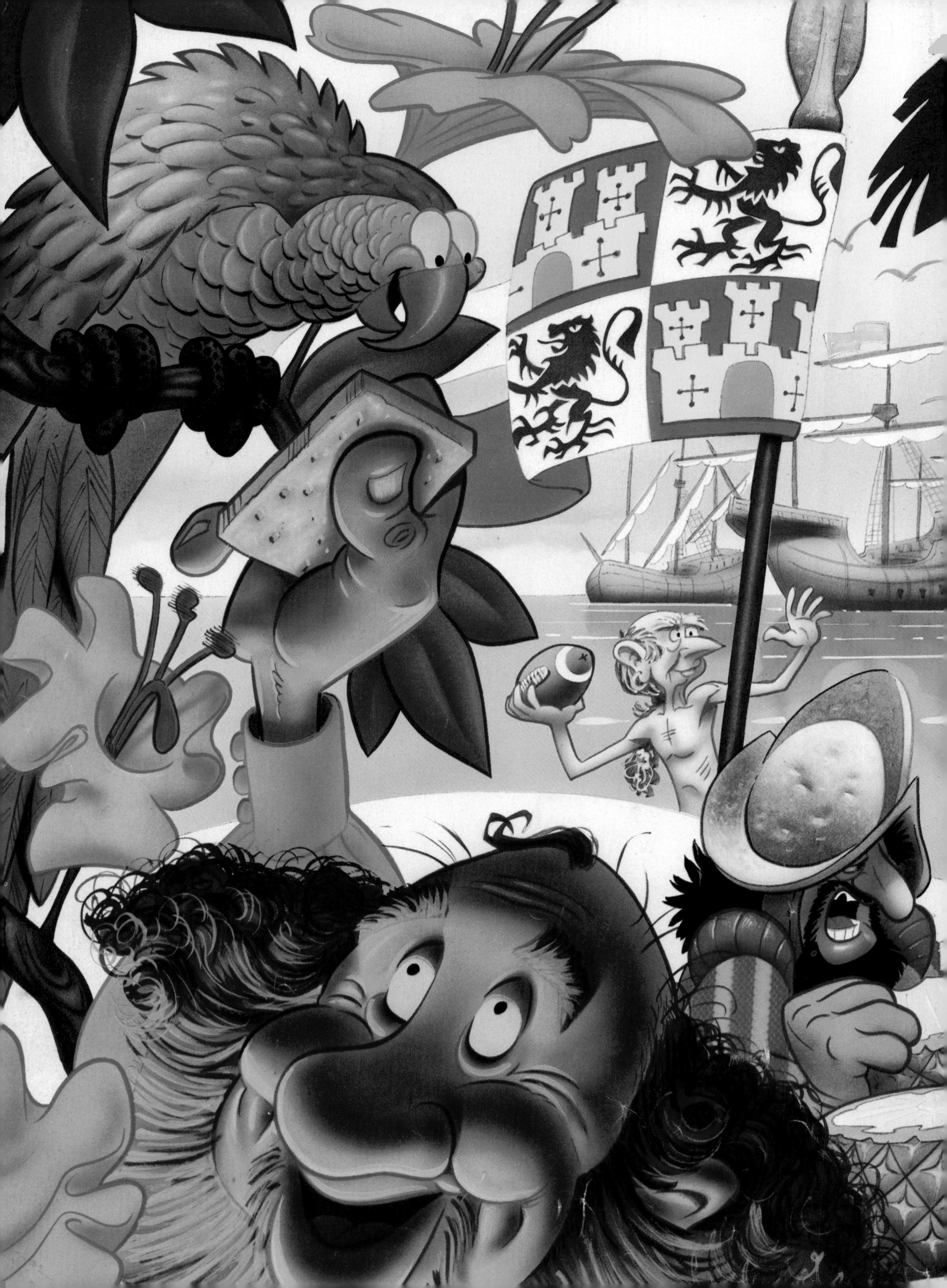

"When it was light, Columbus, Don Pedro, and some of the crew went ashore. Columbus called the island San Salvador and claimed it for the king and queen of Spain.

"The sailors explored the island. They found friendly natives, beautiful parrots, flowers, and fruits. But they didn't find the gold and fabulous cities Columbus was expecting.

" 'China must be around here somewhere,' said Columbus.

" 'No way, Chris,' replied Don Pedro. 'I've been all over this island, and there's not a single Chinese restaurant. If you ask me, we're onto something new here.'

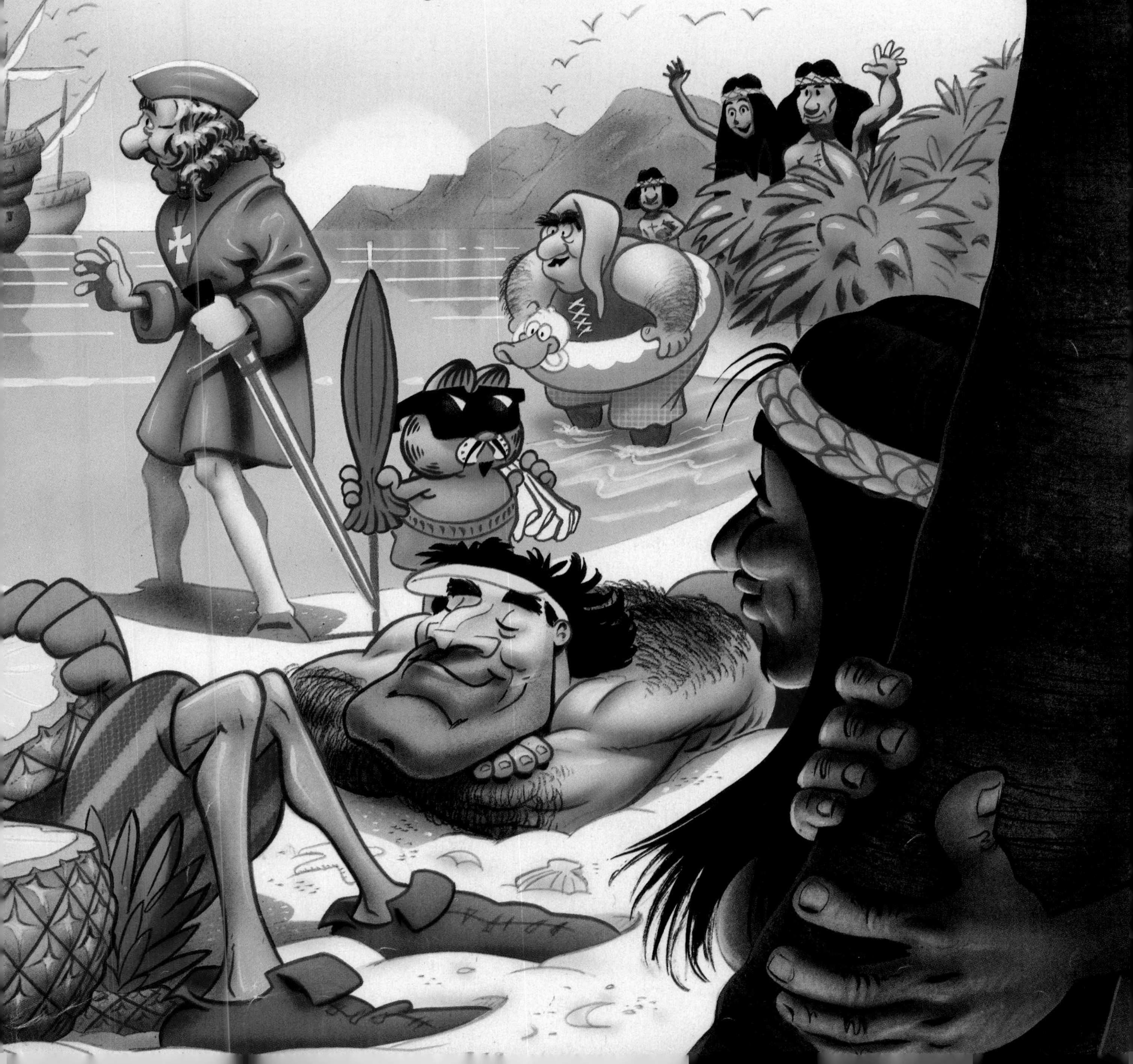

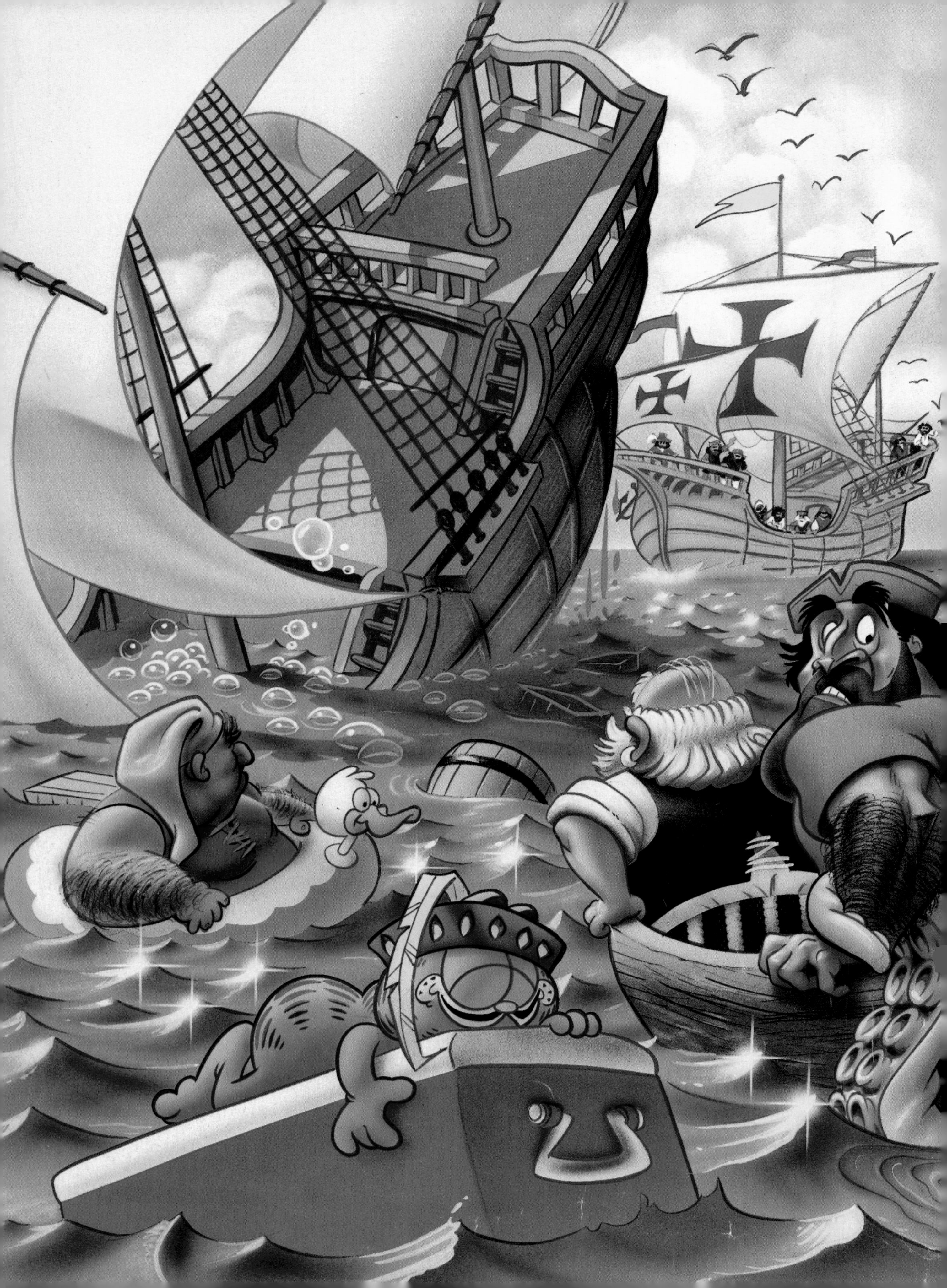

"Leaving San Salvador, Columbus explored two larger islands that we now call Cuba and Haiti. Near Haiti the *Santa María* hit a reef and sank. Fortunately, Don Pedro, Columbus, and the crew escaped unharmed and were picked up by the *Niña*.

"On January 16, 1493, the *Niña* and the *Pinta* began the long voyage home. It was a difficult journey. A terrible storm separated the *Niña* and the *Pinta,* nearly sinking them both.

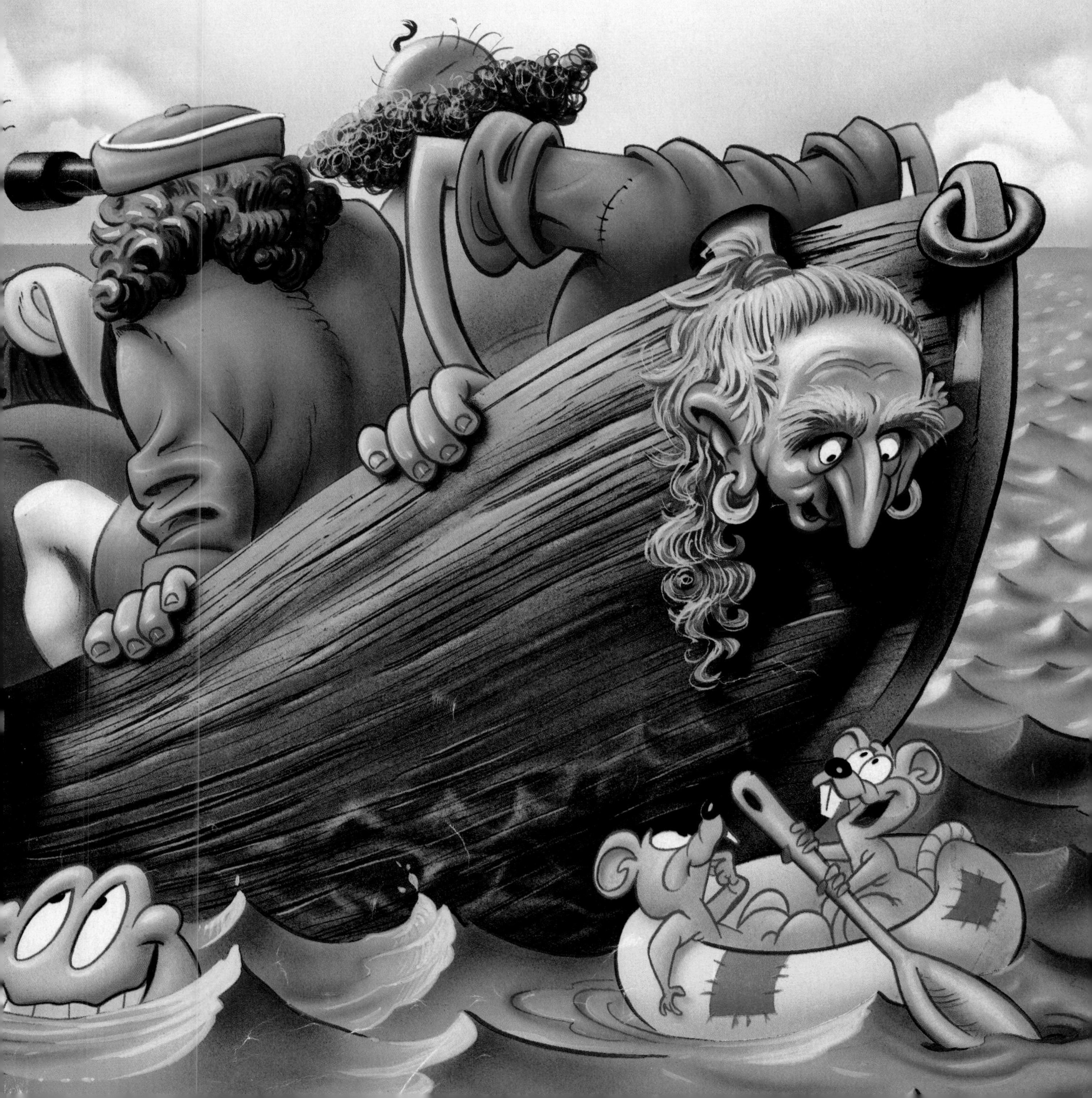

"Finally, on March 15, 1493, Don Pedro Garfield, Columbus, and the battered *Niña* reached the Spanish harbor where the voyage had began. Just by luck, the *Pinta* arrived a short time later.

"All the people turned out to cheer Don Pedro and applaud politely for Columbus. When the two explorers returned to court, Queen Isabella reached out to hug Don Pedro. And King Ferdinand bit his scepter.

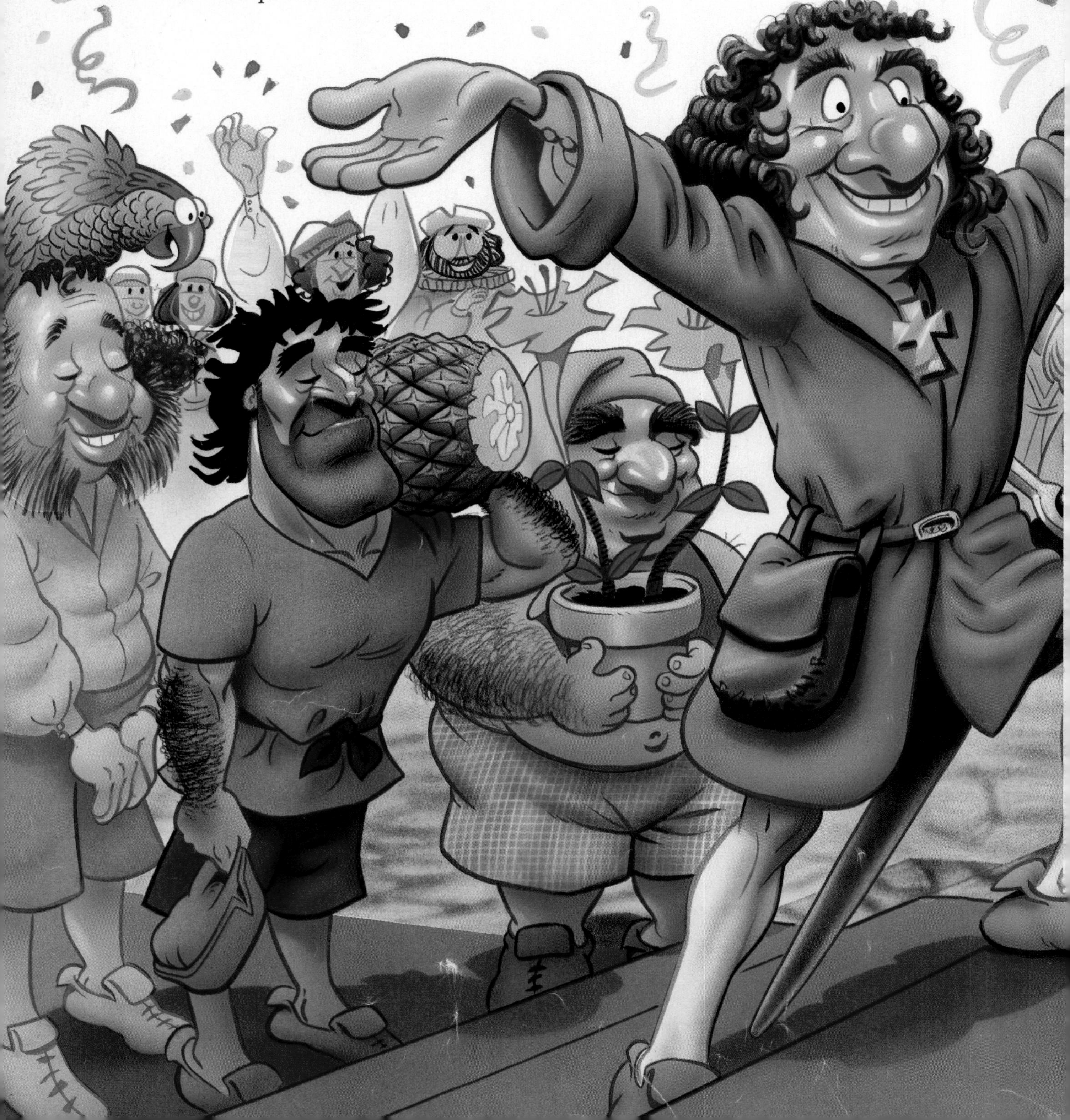

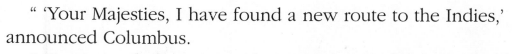

" 'Your Majesties, I have found a new route to the Indies,' announced Columbus.

" 'Don't you believe it,' said Don Pedro Garfield. 'We're talking new world here. It's a nice place, too. Lots of sun, great beaches, plenty of parking. And I've got just the name for it . . .' "

"America?" suggested Nermal.

"Garfieldland," replied Garfield. "Unfortunately, it never caught on. Of course, they didn't name it after Columbus either. Another explorer named Amerigo Vespucci managed to get 'America' printed on all the maps, and it stuck. But I think you can see, Nermal, that it was my brave and determined ancestor, Don Pedro Garfield, who actually discovered America. They ought to set up a statue of him, not Columbus. But history gives humans all the credit."

"Did Columbus ever find the route to China?" asked Nermal.

"The world was a lot bigger than Columbus thought," explained Garfield. "But he only missed China by a little bit. Yeah, like *eight thousand miles!* And this guy gets his own holiday! Can you believe it?"

"Garfield, are you sure that story is all true?"

"I swear it on a stack of pancakes," replied Garfield. "And to prove I know my history, let me tell you another story. It's about my uncle Thomas. You know, the cat who wrote the Declaration of Independence . . ."

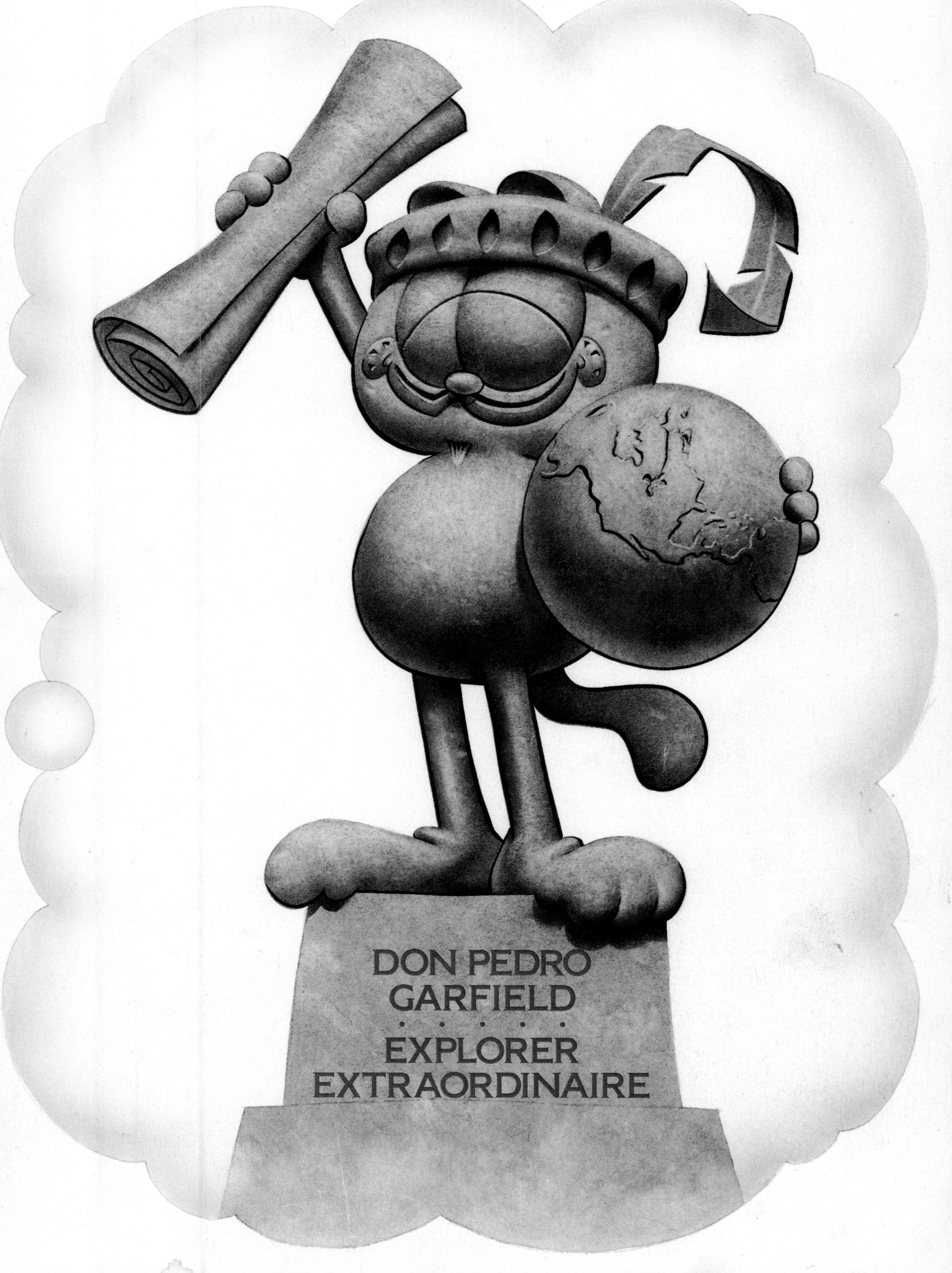
DON PEDRO
GARFIELD
EXPLORER
EXTRAORDINAIRE

In 1492 educated people knew that the world was round. But they were not sure how big it was. It was bigger than Columbus thought. He believed it would take about three weeks to sail from the Canary Islands to China and Japan. But it would have taken him more than three months. He did not know that China and Japan lay farther west, across an unknown continent and another enormous ocean.

Christopher Columbus was a great sailor and dreamer. But he did not realize what an important discovery he had made. He died in 1506, disappointed because the "Indies" he had found were not the wealthy lands he was expecting.

Columbus was not the first person to see America, of course. Native Americans, whom Columbus called Indians, were living in America thousands of years before Columbus arrived. And some Vikings reached North America around A.D. 1000. But Columbus made European explorers aware of America, and the explorers were followed by settlers.

Columbus truly changed the course of history. And who knows? Maybe he had a little help from a cat!

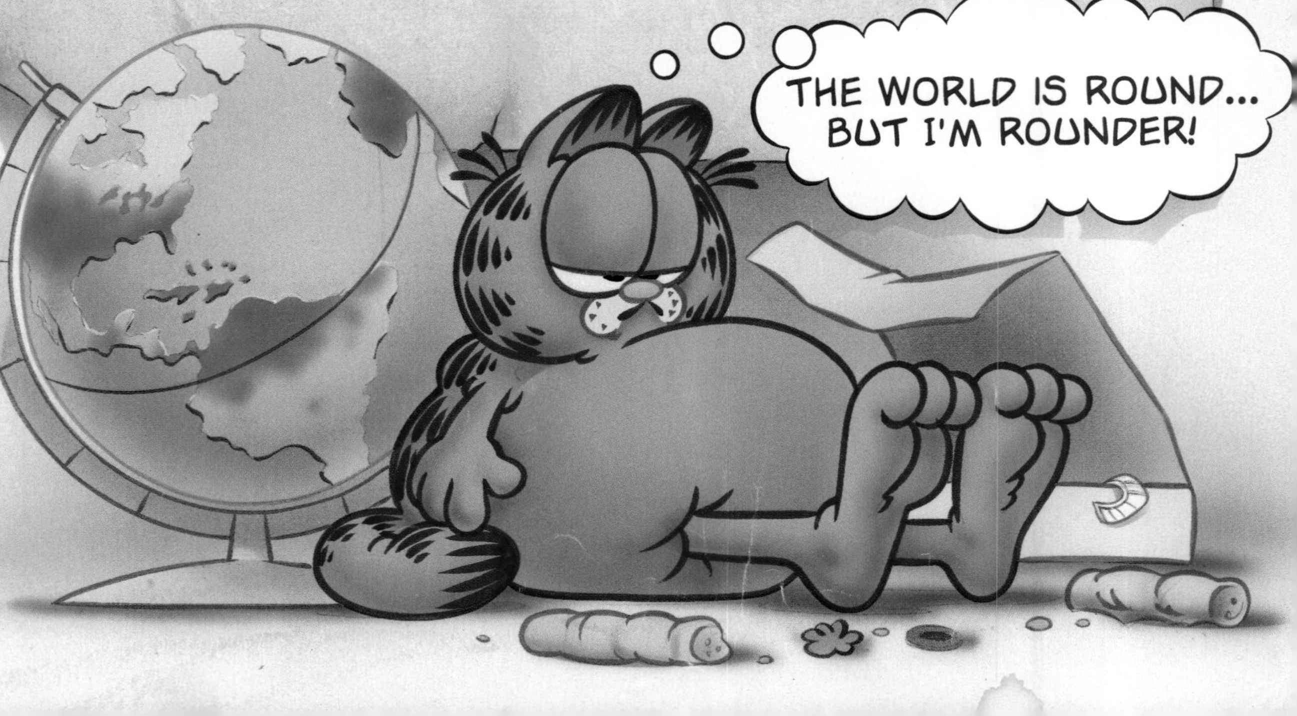
THE WORLD IS ROUND... BUT I'M ROUNDER!

EAU CLAIRE DISTRICT LIBRARY